# The Dilemmas of Being an African American Male in the New Millennium: Solutions for Life Transformation (2<sup>nd</sup> Edition)

*By:*

*Chance W. Lewis, Ph.D.*

*Kris F. Erskine, Th.D.*

i

**Published by:**

LEWIS EDUCATIONAL CONSULTANTS

Lewis Educational Consultants, Inc.
Phone: (704) 659-6842
Fax: (866) 370.2642
Web: http://www.chancewlewis.com
E-mail: chance.lewis@gmail.com

# Dedication

*Chance W. Lewis, Ph.D.*

This book is dedicated to my grandparents, Mr. Lloyd O. Lewis, Sr.; Mrs. Peggy Lewis; Mrs. K. Frances Thomas and Dr. William. W. Clem. I would like to thank you for planting a seed of greatness down in me early in my life that over time nurtured into something great.

Also, this book is dedicated to four great men who "stepped in the gap" to show me the necessary skills I needed to become a man and overcome my own *dilemmas*. Rev. David Williams, senior Pastor of Abyssinian Christian Church in Fort Collins, Colorado, who taught me how to really love God and be a great husband and a great father. To my Uncle Miland Lewis, who taught me that I should always stay connected to my extended family and made sure I did so. To my brother, Tyrone Davis, who taught me how to survive "in the hood," which enabled me to really survive in any environment. Finally, to my best friends Demond Turner, Thomas 'Tommy J' Hutcherson and Timothy Wallace, who taught me how to 'keep it real' in the midst of my life successes. I thank you all for giving me a piece of your lives, so that my life would become better and I could fulfill my destiny.

Finally, I also dedicate this book to my two younger brothers, Olajuwon Davis and Rashad Davis and my sister Comaneci Davis. It is my hope that in some way I have been a positive role model for each of you. Also, I hope that this book will assist you in overcoming your *dilemmas* as you face them on the journey we call life.

# Dedication

*Kris F. Erskine, Th.D.*

This book is dedicated to all the men who have made investments in my life. From my Grandfather-Robert Clark, Sr. to Edward Patrick my football coach at Tuskegee University and my Pastor T.L. Lewis of Birmingham, Alabama. These men along with countless others from barber shops, community centers and classrooms have truly allowed me to make withdrawals from their life account. It is certainly by their advice, assistance and availability that I strive to be the man that I am today.

This book is also dedicated to all those over the course of 20 years of ministry that have allowed me the privilege to mentor them in some capacity. I must say that the assurance that you have in me when at times I could not even see in myself has proven immeasurable in my pursuit for purpose. Just remember that the seeds of greatness planted in you are watered everyday by the spirit of perseverance and determination.

# Acknowledgements

*Chance W. Lewis, Ph.D.*

I want to thank my wife, Mechael B. Lewis and my daughters Myra Nicole Lewis and Sydney Camille Lewis for allocating the room and space for me to complete this monumental project. It is for each of you that I continue to labor on the educational battlefield so that you may have a brighter future. I love you each of you very much!

I also want to acknowledge my mother Mrs. Brenda C. Davis who made many countless sacrifices so I could enjoy "the good life" that this world has to offer. It is because of your many sacrifices that I now have the opportunity to show the world what you already knew I could do since the day I was born. I love you!

Last, but definitely not least, I want to thank my Lord and Savior Jesus Christ. You have brought me through many *dilemmas* and I thank you for allowing me to survive the tests of life and learning to totally trust in you. I want to give you all the praise for the opportunity to write this much needed book and to allow me to untangle some of the many thoughts I have in my head. Max Lucado (2005), one of the nation's best-selling authors states, "when God gives the assignment, he also gives you the skill" (p.2). I thank you God for the assignment at just the right time and the skill set that you have provided that was prepackaged in me since the beginning of time!!

## References

Lucado, M. (2005). *Cure for the common life: Living in your sweet spot.* Nashville, TN: W. Publishing Group.

# Acknowledgements

*Kris F. Erskine, Th.D.*

To My Angel-Mrs. Loretta Erskine, whom I met in August 1995 and who has made great sacrifices to assist me in living my dream-THANK YOU!
It is truly your love and support that fuels me to weather the storms of life with the spirit of excellence. The confidence that the world has come to appreciate about me was developed in the classroom where you allowed me to become the student as you were my teacher!

To Kristian Gabriel and Alayna Gabrielle, my two beautiful children, thank you for allowing the proud privilege of parenting. For all the times we played together and you thought it was me making time for you, I appreciate you letting me share those special moments with you. I needed them more!

To my brother Sidell who has been the beneficiary of my blessings and bruises as big brother. Living with you in my life has allowed the advantage of practicing into perfection. You were my Kristian before he came into existence. Thanks Bro!

Lastly, to my mother-Minister Donno Erskine, who endured embarrassment, ridicule and fear to provide me with the ability to seize opportunities of a lifetime. Thank you for exposure! "Variety is the spice of life." I never forgot that! To every single-parent, I am proof positive that you can do it!

## References

The State of Black America 2007- National Urban League
Wikipedia- The Middle Passage

# Preface

## At the Crossroads of Destiny and Current Reality: The Dilemmas of Being an African American Male in the United States

*Chance W. Lewis, Ph.D. and Kris F. Erskine, Th.D.*

In the 2nd edition of this highly successful book, we revisit the unique dynamic of being an African American male in today's society. We start off this book with the famous words of W.E.B. DuBois, "how does it feel to be a problem?" As we examine the current landscape of American society, African American males continue to garner serious media attention and the national spotlight not for the many positive contributions that are made on a daily basis but for negative stories and headlines that are many times manufactured to get likes and clicks. However, we must understand that African American males are more valuable than these superficial barometers. Unfortunately, we often hear the notion that African American males are in crisis! However, for the 2nd edition of this book, we propose to change the narrative from African American males being in a state of crisis to "how society treats African American men through flawed systems, policies, and lack of opportunities that is at the foundation of the crisis. We must understand that a prevailing narrative continues to exist to devalue the African American male in many ways with the ultimate goal of removing this population from their families, communities, opportunities for advance and ultimately not being able to achieve what they were destined to be.

We want to make it crystal clear that African American males are not menaces to society that just wake up to commit crimes. Thousands and thousands of African

American males wake up each and everyday to serve their God, provide for their families and pursue life, liberty and the pursuit of happiness! Unfortunately, in today's society, any African American male that does not live a life of crime in the United States is seen as an exception to this rule. To change the narrative, we must understand that African American males continue to make outstanding achievements in today's society. We list a few just for the sake of example purposes. While this list is definitely not exhaustive, it paints a picture of everyday African American males that are putting a positive footprint on society.

| | |
|---|---|
| Te-Nehisi Coats (42 years old) | Prolific Author; sold millions of copies of his books; Featured on The Oprah Winfrey Show |
| Jahkil Jackson (10 years old) | This young man from Chicago sent 2017 crafting 5,000 blessing bags full of necessities for the city's homeless population and was recognized by President Barack Obama. |
| Brandon Frame (41 years old) | Celebrates Men & Boys of Color. Started *The Black Man Can* on Instagram. Started a blog in 2010 that has evolved into a series of programs, workshops, social media campaigns each inspiring and awe-striking for positive reasons. |
| Sterling Brown (41 years old) | Became the first Black man to win the award for outstanding male actor in a drama series in the SAG |

| | |
|---|---|
| | Awards, as well as the first Black man to win a Golden Globe for a TV drama. |
| Ryan Coogler (31 years old) | Director of the Blockbuster Movie, *Black Panther* |

Source: Insider.com

In addition to these great names, there are countless other African American males that are changing society for the better.

Unfortunately, over the past few years, as cell phone videos have become more popular, we have seen more disturbing footage of Black men being killed at the hands of law-enforcement officers. Here is a list of 50 African American men that we remember as we dig deeper into this topic.

| |
|---|
| Jimmy Atchinson (21 years old) |
| Willie McCoy (20 years old) |
| Emantic "EJ" Fitzgerald Bradford, Jr. (21 years old) |
| D'ettrick Griffin (18 years old) |
| Jemel Roberson (26 years old) |
| DeAndre Ballard (23 years old) |
| Botham Shem Jean (26 years old) |
| Antwon Rose Jr. (17 years old) |
| Robert Lawrence White (41 years old) |
| Anthony Lamar Smith (24 years old) |
| Ramarley Graham (18 years old) |
| Manuel Loggins Jr. (31 years old) |
| Travon Martin (17 years old) |
| Wendell Allen (20 years old) |
| Kendrec McDade (19 years old) |
| Larry Jackson Jr. (32 years old) |
| Jonathan Ferrell (24 years old) |
| Jordan Baker (26 years old) |
| Victor White III (22 years old) |
| Dontre Hamilton (31 years old) |

Eric Garner (43 years old)
John Crawford III (22 years old)
Michael Brown (18 years old)
Ezell Ford (25 years old)
Dante Parker (36 years old)
Kajieme Powell (25 years old)
Laquan McDonald (17 years old)
Akai Gurley (28 years old)
Tamir Rice (12 years old)
Rumain Brisbon (34 years old)
Jerame Reid (36 years old)
Charly Keunang (43 years old)
Tony Robinson (19 years old)
Walter Scott (50 years old)
Freddie Gray (25 years old)
Brendon Glenn (29 years old)
Samuel DuBose (43 years old)
Christian Taylor (19 years old)
Jamar Clark (24 years old)
Mario Woods (26 years old)
Quintonio LeGrier (19 years old)
Gregory Gunn (58 years old)
Akiel Denkins (24 years old)
Alton Sterling (37 years old)
Philando Castile (32 years old)
Terrance Sterling (31 years old)
Terence Crutcher (40 years old)
Keith Lamont Scott (43 years old)
Alfred Olango (38 years old)
Jordan Edwards (15 years old)

Source: NewsOne

As a result of these few examples, many African American males are still at the crossroads of what we call a *dilemma* as to what path their life will take in the U.S. especially during the Trump era. The questions we posted in the first edition of this book still hold true today: (a) Will the lives of African American males be filled with the prosperity that is promised to every citizen in the United States; (b) Will the lives of African American males take a path where they will never be fully embraced no matter what type of accomplishments they will make?; (c) Does this society have a glass ceiling on what the African American male will be able to do based on the structure of this society?

We still hold the position that it is unfortunate that men who were involuntarily brought to the United States as slaves, to toil and labor to build the infrastructure of this great country, are still treated as second-class or sometimes even third-class citizens. Even with all of the great accomplishments that African American men have had in the United States of America, we are still described in many circles with the following adjectives: (a) dysfunctional; (b) drug dealers; (c) pimps; (d) murderers, (e) hyper-sexual; (f) athletic but not intelligent; (g) savages; (h) absentee fathers; (i) dead-beat dads; (j) prisoners; (k) substance abusers; (l) poor; (m) welfare dependent; (n) unemployable; (o) underemployed; (p) a detriment to the community; and many other characteristics. As a result, the African American male continually faces many *dilemmas* or what W.E.B. Dubois (1903) refers to as double-consciousness as we try to navigate what it means to be an African American male in a country that in many ways does not even value our existence.

In conclusion, the 2nd edition of this book is truly an act of God, who has brought two men together, from different professions, from different states, to speak about the current plight of every African American male who are facing the daily *dilemmas* of this life. From the story of Adam and Even in the Garden of Eden, with a *dilemma* of whether or not Adam should eat fruit from the tree of knowledge of good and evil or the brother who is trying to decide if he should continue on a job that is paying him less than he knows he deserves or turn to a life of crime to take care of his family. Wherever we, as African American males are in these spectra of *dilemmas*, we hope this book will serve as a roadmap to help you reach the Will that God has for your life.

## References

DuBois, W.E.B. (1903). *The souls of Black folk.* New York: Random House.

Insider (2019). 20 Black people who are making history in 2018. Washington, DC: Author.

NewsOne (2019). *56 Black Men and Boys Killed by Police.* Washington, DC: Author.

Obama, B. (2007). Foreward. In National Urban League (Eds.), *The State of Black America* (pp. 9-12).

Webster, M. (2007). On-Line Dictionary. Available at http://www.merriam-webster.com/

# CONTENTS

# PART II – THE SOLUTIONS

## Introduction

# The Systematic Elimination of African American Males: Does Anyone Care?

*Chance W. Lewis, Ph.D.*

Presently, the reality of the plight of the African American male continues to be very clear that all of these dilemmas faced are not by happenstance; they are systematic! Let's be clear, the African American male is disappearing right before our eyes. Unfortunately, it now happens so much that we as a society has become numb to its seriousness. In our current society, this reality is before us on a daily basis when we watch the local, state, regional or national news on our various smart devices. Ironically, it still does not matter what city or state we live in or near, the story is the same, an African American male died over something as simple as what he was wearing, a drug deal gone bad, a female he was dating, retaliation for an earlier crime he committed or just mistaken identity. Or, even the most famous one, "he fit a description of someone law enforcement was looking for." Given that this phenomenon is tearing away at the fabric of the African American community and many other communities across the United States, the following questions are warranted:

How do we (those who are genuinely concerned) put a stop to this issue?

Where do we even start?

What policy issues need to be addressed?

Who will lead this effort?

Who can we bring aboard to partner in our efforts?

Who is willing to lend a helping hand?

We must understand this fight to save the African American male will have to be done by those who are genuinely concerned. This is clearly evident because many people in our society have found ways to capitalize from the high death and incarceration rates of the African American male. The prison industry has become big business on Wall Street. Privately owned corporate entities such as Visa, American Express, and many other corporate sponsors have secretly made millions of dollars on this *new slavery* inside the prison system, which is mainly populated by African American males and other males of color. This is still unfortunate because until recently the African American male college population has just exceeded the African American male prison population (Toldson, 2019). Unfortunately, this should not even be a comparison that we have to make.

To paint an even bleaker picture, many researchers and policy makers have provided data to illustrate that the African American male is dying at a rate that exceeds his African American female counterparts, thus drawing even larger implications for the African American community. Also, when comparing the death rates to their White male and female counterparts, the African American male is dying at rates that far exceed this group as well. As a case in point, the National Urban League (2018) provides data from the Equality Index on the death rates of African American males. The data is as follows:

Table 1

*Death Rates for African American males per 100,000 people*

| Death Rates per 100,000 people | African American males | White males |
|---|---|---|
| Ages 1-14 | 2.4 | 1.2 |
| Ages 15-24 | 93.3 | 17.7 |
| Ages 25-34 | 96.5 | 22.1 |
| Ages 35-44 | 57.6 | 22.7 |
| Ages 45-64 | 21.5 | 24.0 |

Source: National Urban League (2018)

In Table 1, we find data that clearly illustrates that at every age category, African American males exceed their counterparts by a significant margin. This is especially alarming given that these death rates of males tear away at the fabric of the African American community. While these numbers may seem straightforward in Table 1, the complexities of these numbers are revealed in so many lives that are not as easily displayed in a table. More specifically, this means that when African American males die young, they are not able to be fathers for their children, husbands for African American women, and role models in the community. We must ask ourselves, does anyone even care?

Next, as we seek to examine the plight of the vanishing African American male, we find the following related to deaths resulting from firearm-related deaths:

Table 2

*2018 Fire-Arm Related Deaths (All Ages, All Males) per 100,000 people*

| Age | African American Males | White Males |
|-----|------------------------|-------------|
| 1-14 | 2.0 | 0.7 |
| 15-24 | 80.7 | 14.3 |
| 25-44 | 59.2 | 17.4 |
| 35-44 | 83.6 | 16.9 |
| 45-64 | 18.3 | 19.2 |
| 65+ | 14.6 | 27.6 |

Source: National Urban League (2018)

As we see in Table 2, firearms have had a tremendous impact on the vanishing of the African American male. Table 2 illustrates that African American males lead the death rates for firearms in comparison to White males in the following categories: Ages 1-14, 15-24, 25-34, and 35-44. This is devastating given the fact that the majority of these crimes are considered Black-on-Black crime. However, the main question is: Does anyone even care that this is going on in the African American community?

Finally, as we set the stage for this important book, we must understand that death rates are not the only phenomenon or *dilemma* affecting the African American community. The high incarceration rates have had a tremendous impact as well. Table 3 provides information detailing when African American males and White males commit the same crime, African American males will

4

receive prison sentences that are disproportionate to their White male counterparts.

Table 3

*Average Prison Sentence for African American Males and White Males (in Months)*

| Offense | Average Months-African American Males | Average Months-White Males |
|---|---|---|
| Sexual Assault | 125 | 115 |
| Robbery | 101 | 89 |
| Aggravated Assault | 48 | 42 |
| Burglary | 25 | 21 |
| Burglary | 44 | 37 |

Source: National Urban League (2018)

Given the data in Table 3, it is clearly evident that the disparities in prison sentences between African American males and White males illustrate that the "justice for all" section in the Pledge of Allegiance to the United States is not given out fairly. As a result, the vanishing of the African American male is greatly impacted by our justice system as well. As previously mentioned, does anyone care?

As we prepare you, the reader, to peruse through this book, the constant question that overrides this entire volume are as follows:

Do you care?

What will you do to make a difference in the lives of African American males who are vanishing right before our eyes?

It is our hope that you do care and you will do your part to make a change in the lives of a population that is calling out for our help. We have attempted in this book to do something that many other books and authors fall short of doing. First, we present the issues that have African American males on the brink of extinction such as: (a) His Vertical Relationship with God; (b) the Horizontal relationships with his family; (c) the importance of educational attainment; (d) unemployment and underemployment issues (e) substance abuse; and (f) economic issues.

However, different from other authors, we provide a section in this book that is focused specifically on solutions with each of the following chapters: (a) repairing the vertical relationship with God; (b) mending the relationships with his family; (c) improving educational attainment; (d) strategies for improving the unemployment and underemployment issue; (e) overcoming substance abuse and reclaiming your life; and (f) getting your money--the right way.

We hope this book will serve as a call to action for everyone that is genuinely concerned with the *dilemmas* that African American males face on a daily basis. More importantly, we hope this book will provide the evidence needed for you to play a part in documenting African American males in your community are vanishing. God has allowed this book to come forward at this specific time to complete a great work. God continue to bless you and keep you.

# References

Toldson, I. (2019). *No BS (Bad Stats): Black people need people who believe in Black people enough not to believe every bad thing they hear about Black people.* New York: Brill – Sense.

# The Issues

# Chapter 1

# The Vertical Relationship with God

"You impress at a distance, but you impact a life up close.
The closer the relationship the greater the impact."
**Howard Hendricks**

*Kris F. Erskine, Th.D.*

What's Going On"...are the famous words to the tune
elegantly sung by R&B crooner and Motown legend
Marvin Gaye. With introspective lyrics about drug abuse,
poverty and the Vietnam War, the album was an immediate
sensation and has endured as a classic of early-1970s soul.
His words seem somewhat prophetic as we examine the
instability of the generations past and present. The great
falling away can best be categorized by the abandonment of
the one-time absolutes in the African American
community. It is visible from the lack of respect of
heritage and for self, to the failure to place emphasis on
education, and minimizing the majors. We are a positional
people, with direction and distinction. I personally believe
that the demise of a people is a persistent progression away
from the "ancient landmarks." What are the ancient
landmarks, you may ask?

The Ancient Landmarks like prayer, going to church on
Sunday and eating together as we swap stories as we pass
dishes. I learned to pray a simple prayer- "Now I lay me
down to sleep. I pray the Lord my soul to keep. And If I
should die before I wake, I pray the Lord my soul to take."
Yes, simple but sincere. Going to church on Sunday was
not an option, it was our obligation. The importance of the
Black Church was not a "Sunday thing," but rather a staple
in the fabric of the community.

The church served in a multifarious manner for not only spiritual needs, but educational, social, and financial. The gathering for "Sunday dinner" allowed for fellowship to take place. It fostered fellowship in the regard that it brought the family together in the same place at the same time. A time that was critically important because the family maintained its devotion to the Vertical Relationship with God. It was critical because we received updates about things that pertained to our family and our house. The Vertical Relationship with God had its foundation here. But, seemingly through financial advancements, lack of prioritizing, and loss of values we have abandoned that way of life. The loss of values and the misappropriation of morals that support the porch on which generations have sat and told stories of old as if they were brand new. The constant eroding of the spirit of pride in our culture via colloquialisms that equipped us with the handles to reach one plateau of success after the other are now a distant memory. Handles that brought from segregation to integration. From the back of the bus to owning the bus companies. From "share-cropping" to successful-corporations. It is the Vertical Relationship with God that serves as the mortar between the bricks that allowed the wall of reinforcement to have rest. These walls of reinforcement had its origin in the hearts of grandmothers and fathers who desired for us much more than what they had. In hearts that have been broken by the neglect of the importance of self-appreciation and validation in oneself. In hearts that leak tears due to an emotional breakdown from a present nightmare from past dreams.

For example, it is found in the hands of "hard work" and the tenacity to commit to a menial task to produce millions of opportunities for others. In those same hands that are now callous due to the spirit of determination because of the lack of educational avenues. The Vertical Relationship with God was passed down to us from those same hearts

10

and hands carefully and cautiously. From Africa to America we brought our God! Even when we were not afforded the privilege to pack our clothes or our valuables, we brought our God! It was that same relationship that sustained us through the "Middle of Passage."

The Middle Passage was the longest, hardest, most dangerous, and also most horrific part of the journey of the slave ships. The dreadful place where many lost their lives and others who heroically gave their lives in an attempt of faith to take advantage of that relationship. Bound by chains, they understood what the great theologian Tertullian said – "The legs feel nothing in locks, when the heart is in heaven." Quintus Septimius Florens Tertullianus, anglicized as Tertullian, (ca. 155–230) was a church leader and prolific author of Early Christianity. He also was a notable early Christian apologist. Tertullian, a Romanized African,[1] was born, lived and died in Carthage, in what is today Tunisia. Most contemporary historians estimate that between 9.4 and 12 million Africans arrived in the new world. Diseases and starvation due to the length of the passage were the main contributors to the death toll with amoebic dysentery and scurvy causing the majority of deaths.

It was the place where millions died perhaps grasping solace in prayer to their God. Perhaps it was the Pygmy Prayer or Kikuyu Peace Prayer and/or the Ashanti Prayer for Blessing. Stories are told of how slaves prayed for each other and gave words during ceremonial death services aboard slave ships. It was during this time that even in the face of death, life emerged and babies were born! They held firmly to that relationship when we arrived on the shores of slavery. Whatever the status of these first Africans to arrive at Jamestown, it is clear that by 1640, at least one African had been declared a slave.

This African was ordered by the court "to serve his said master or his assigns for the time of his natural life here or elsewhere." It was evident in the fields from the songs of suffering produced by pain that were sung in the key of hope!

Songs such as

Steal Away-

*Steal away, steal away!*

*Steal away to Jesus!*

*Steal away, steal away home!*

*I ain't got long to stay here!*

This spiritual song was sung by Nat Turner as a signal. Nat, a slave from Virginia, who organized a slave revolt against slave owners, used this song to alert other slaves to meetings.

After the failed revolt and Nat's death, slaves everywhere were forbidden to speak his name. It was, however, worked into the lyrics of another slave song, because of the Vertical Relationship with God. A relationship that was dedicated to the Master above the one here on earth. Far above the one who abused, to the one who would never abandon. For He had promised "to never leave them nor forsake them." It was vibrant in the desire to be free. To be whom we were before we arrived here, FREE! Free to make our own choices and decisions. Free to develop our families with heritage and holiness. Free to be Kings, Queens, Princes, and Princesses. The songs of freedom where drenched in bath of belief, that a better day was coming. It is also apparent in the song; Wade in the Water.

12

Harriet Tubman sang this spiritual as a warning to runaway slaves. To escaping slaves, the song told them to abandon the path and move into the water. By traveling along the water's edge or across a body of water, the slaves would throw chasing dogs and their keepers off the scent.

*Chorus:*

*Wade in the water,*

*Wade in the water children.*

*Wade in the water*

*God's gonna trouble the water.......*

*Who's all those children all dressed in Red?*

*God's gonna trouble the water.*

*Must be the ones that Moses led.*

*God's gonna trouble the water.*

It was with that brilliance that they created an account called "freedom" that the God they trusted as Father would make deposits in. That account is in danger of being overdrawn with broken promises and the attitude of ungratefulness. It is being overdrawn by the senseless murders of the innocent and the disadvantaged. It is being overdrawn by electing not to train a generation whose minds are just as bright as anyone else.

The account called "freedom" is running low because for every student we have in college today, there are 3 in

13

prison. We have now replaced our Vertical Relationship with God with materialism and manufactured happiness. A broken model that will never produce joy in the lives of those connected to it. We have traded character for cars, heritage for houses, and morals for money. We will do anything at any time with anybody for any price. Whatever happened to having dreams of a better day? The challenge of looking beyond our right now into the future of what will become. The words of Langston Hughes yet ring in my ear:

What happens to a dream deferred?

Does it dry up
like a raisin in the sun?
Or fester like a sore--
And then run?
Does it stink like rotten meat?
Or crust and sugar over--
like a syrupy sweet?

Maybe it just sags
like a heavy load.

Or does it explode?

Have we become like the raisin in the sun? Have we become dried from the lack of attention to the foundational truths that provide longevity? Or have we become infectious like the sore with black on black crime. The top 10 deadliest cities, from west coast to east coast, point directly to our neighborhoods as the source of mayhem and murder. It is that gang warfare and "thug" mentality that promotes division among a generation past and the one present. A divide where children are rebelling by the concept of a life that is fictitious at best. That same divide that has parents screaming in frustration over how and when we arrived in this "strange land." A land where criticism from children that cuts to the core. A land where purposeless parents are a threat our children's future. How do we explain this to those millions who have paid on the account called "freedom" and established the Vertical Relationship with God? The millions of trendsetters that died in the "Middle Passage." The countless number of individuals who lost their lives during slavery. The many who died for speaking up for those whose voices have been taken away: Dr. Martin L. King, Jr., Malcolm X, Mary McLeod Bethune, and Fannie Lou Hamer. At present, we are a resourceful community that is now hemorrhaging from a Dream Deferred or Deserted? Who have we become? Could it be that we are a threat to ourselves and to the world? We are the only race of people in jeopardy of destroying itself. We must reclaim the Vertical Relationship and re-establish its priorities and principles. We must begin to train the next set of leaders from our community to speak and stand for the masses. Dr. Na'im Akbar said- "The primary objective of freeing the Black mind is to change the consciousness of black people."

My mother raised me in the rough housing projects with no transportation as she worked relentlessly on her B.A. degree from Tuskegee University, former Tuskegee Institute. We would walk to the store and pray for a ride back home. I can remember asking my mom when we would leave home, "How are we going to get back?" She would always say just trust God. And sure enough He would. This created in me an insatiable attitude even to this day to be determined even in doubtful situations. She instilled in me that Vertical Relationship to God. I would hear her pray when food was scarce, "Lord make a way out of no way." I would see her praise God when she successfully made the Dean's List. I understood early that education and opportunity would always shake hands. But, it was the confidence in a God that I could not see who would make the difference. It is that same mindset I have developed with my own family. Set my own priorities in life and examine God's hand of deliverance bringing me in and out of situations that are paramount to my success today. It is when we look up to God and cast all of our cares upon him we find out that he really does care about us!

## 2nd Edition Reflections

The Vertical Relationship with God for men, especially African American men, is of most importance. According to Cathy Grossman of USA Today, "Women outnumber men in attendance in every major Christian denomination, and they are 20% to 25% more likely to attend worship at least weekly." The 2001 US Congregational Life Survey (USCLS) reinforces this very data. This survey revealed that an average American congregation is roughly 61% female and 39% male. In 2008 when the 1st Edition of Dilemmas was published, my philosophical position on this subject was from a very limited and minute perspective. An inexperienced husband, young and naïve father of a son 8 and a daughter 3, and transitioning from the south to the north for better opportunities. Now, some 11 years advanced, life has not only confirmed but challenged the necessity of this vertical relationship with God. The demographics of our declining society is proof positive that we live in trying times. The constant demands on men to produce, provide, and protect those he loves seems as a never ending transition. Most men have an epiphany during a transition of their lives. It is in these rare, but regarded moments, we reflect on what was and the will be. We evaluate in secret and silence. It is here we find safety and a non-judgmental zone, where we are accountable to a select few. We wrestle within to find the answers to questions that keep seemingly slipping through our hands. Sounds familiar?

Well, there was a certain man name Jacob, who had mastered the art of manipulation. He had taken advantage of every relationship afforded to him. He is what Dr. George Simon describes in his book- "In Sheep's Clothing: Understanding and Dealing with Manipulative People"- a covert aggressive. Dr. Simon further expresses, "If you're dealing with a person who rarely gives you a straight answer to a straight question, is always making excuses for doing hurtful things, tries to make you feel guilty, or uses any of the other tactics to throw you on the defensive and get their way, you can assume you're dealing with a person who- no matter what else he/or she may be- is covertly aggressive.

Jacob lied to his father to swindle something of substance that rightfully belonged to his brother. He coerced his mother to assist him against his father and in doing so damaged their relationship because of greed and selfishness. He later relocates because his brother is furious at the revelation of his actions. His mother's desire to save his life is greater than repairing it, and sends him to her brother, his uncle's home for hiding. Jacob is away from home, but not away from Jacob. His fatal mistake is shone in the absences of a true Vertical Relationship. Jacob's deficiency is demonstrated in the common dilemma many men suffer from- "ESCAPAGE" from reality. Our fantasy life is far more enjoyable than our real one. He concocts a plan to deceive his uncle of his possessions as well. Manipulators have no filter. Taking advantage of any situation seems normal to them. But as providence would have it, his uncle is master manipulator too. He makes a promise to his nephew with intentions of keeping his word. Through disappointment and determination, Jacob will not be outdone. After having spent some twenty years in his uncle's home, he is commanded to return to the land of his ancestors. He leaves behind a trail of brokenness because hurt people inevitably hurt people.

In order to return, he must pass through the territory of his brother. They have not spoken in over twenty years. Their last conversation exploded with anger and justified hostility. Jacob does what most insecure men do, he ran away hoping to never face the issue again. But, as God would design it, before Jacob's horizontal relationship with those he has hurt is repaired, he must address the Vertical Relationship with God he abandoned years ago. As anxiety amplifies Jacob is restless and weary at the very thought of facing his brother. His only companion for the night is a series of questions....

"What will happen when we finally see each other?"
"Will he react in rage?"
"What should I say to him?"
"Are thoughts of killing me still prevalent on his mind?"
"Has bitterness eradicated the possibility of forgiveness?"

Have you asked yourself any of the questions?

His Vertical Relationship with God now demands attention. The story states that he was left alone. It is here that true hurt and healing face another. Each wound is stared down by wholeness. If Jacob is ever going to bring balance to his life, he must address the abandonment of the Vertical Relationship with God. After wrestling with his aloneness, he understands now that this is the most important relationship we can have. Jacob realized what all men who submit to God have and that is we are not complete without Him. We are not complete in any other area when God is "vertically challenged" in our lives. True assessment is accomplished when we left alone with our creator.

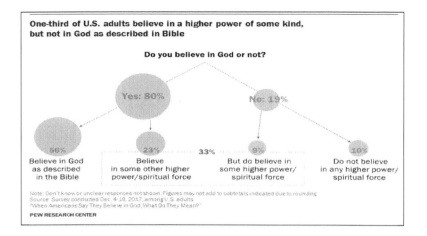

The chart provides interesting data on this subject.
56% - Believe in God as described in the Bible
23% - Believe in some other higher power/spiritual force
9%  - Do not believe in God, but in some higher power
10% - Do not believe in any higher power/ spiritual force

Which category are you presently in? Are you satisfied with your position and belief system? Decisions made in the Vertical Relationship will affect the outcome of your Horizontal Relationship each time.

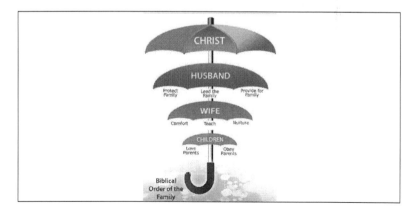

CHRIST
HUSBAND
Protect Family     Lead the Family     Provide for Family
WIFE
Comfort     Teach     Nurture
CHILDREN
Love Parents     Obey Parents
Biblical Order of the Family

Decisions made in the Vertical Relationship that will affect the outcome of your Horizontal Relationship each time.

# Chapter 2

# The Horizontal Relationship with His Family

"The horizontal frame of relationships will be described locally at various levels. In a family, every member will occupy a specific social niche, such as in a holistic view for the family unit to be functional." HORIZONTAL AND VERTICAL SOCIAL RELATIONSHIP- by Florian Colceag

*"I have no wish to play the pontificating fool, pretending that I've suddenly come up with the answers to all life's questions. Quite the contrary, I began this book as an exploration, an exercise in self-questioning. In other words, I wanted to find out, as I looked back at a long and complicated life, with many twists and turns, how well I've done at measuring up to the values I myself have set." -* **From Sidney Poitier's book The Measure of a Man.**

*Kris F. Erskine, Th.D.*

I must concur that Poitier is correct that life is long and complicated and, yes, it is filled with twists and turns. But the true measure of a man is honesty with himself. The truth of the matter is that African American males have dilemmas...from juggling schedules to provide support, to insecurities that invade our own insight, to silent struggles that stare at us from the private portals of our past. We must admit that we are not Superman - the fictional hero ready to save the day, but rather Clark Kent. The contrast between the two is amazing in research because while different they are the same person. Clark Kent is the ordinary man who walks, talks just as all men do. But, it is the secret that he is also Superman, that gives life and fulfillment to Clark Kent. He wears underneath his suit and tie "the Superman suit." He is always in touch with his

21

alter-ego. The underlying factor is to never confuse the two. Clark was weak for Lois and Superman although possessing superabundant strength was weak to kryptonite.

Like Clark Kent, most men find themselves in the *dilemma* of trying to act out heroic situations with the desire of Superman, but in reality, all we are really is Clark Kent. There are some things in life that overtake us and find us off guard. Those challenges of losing a job, failing a class, lack of finances, and others too numerous to name, rob us of fantasy for reality. It is when we can admit this apparent fact that we can come face to face with the kryptonite that cripples us.

Oswald Chambers once said, "We are in danger of forgetting that we cannot do what God does, and that God will not do what we can do."

One day Jesus was on a mountaintop in ministry class with his core group of disciples while the others wrestled with a dad who had a *dilemma*. This man's son was a danger to himself as well as others. The Bible recorded that he often found himself in jeopardy, of falling into the water, and into the fire. This father brought his son with high hopes of finding a cure for his crisis only to find that no help was available.

I understand the hardships applied to the lives of those of us who dare to be called African American males. Seven years ago, I watched my son fight for his life in a neonatal intensive care unit as a premature baby weighing only 2.5 pounds. The feelings of helplessness did not overshadow my spirit of hopefulness. My belief that God would answer prayer provided me with strength to find shelter in my sudden storm. I, too - like the Father above - sought assistance from others only to find that in life there are some episodes that you must stand on center stage alone.

For every African American male who is battling the spirit of sorrow and depths of despair, I encourage you to persevere in the power of God's purpose for your life. I had to learn that real men do cry sometimes, and that tears are God's way of clearing the path of perception for powerful people. My first Father's Day found my son still some months later in the neonatal intensive care unit, but vastly improving and preparing to come home. The hurt and disappointment I felt, not to mention the inner turmoil, and my personal fight with a fatigue of faith, caused me to develop an attitude of gratitude. I challenged myself to press beyond that scenario in my life and count my many blessings and name them one by one.

The father in the Scripture became inspiration to me because he did not settle, but rather waited until Jesus ended class where he could have a one-on-one session with him. After a personal conversation with Jesus, I must admit that two miracles occurred that day: one in the saving of the son and the other in the soul of Dad. It was then that he, just as I, found that in our *dilemmas* as dads, God may not come when we want him to, but he is always on time!

## 2nd Edition Reflections

Our son, Kristian, absolutely, unequivocally, and unashamedly loves Marvel movies and characters. His passion for them is where I drew inspiration and insight on this subject. He has committed me to each major Marvel movie and reminds me of the release date months in advance. He studies the characters as if his pen wrote the script. After a conversation with him, in the first edition of Dilemmas of Being African American Male, I mentioned the "Clark Kent vs. Superman Syndrome."

After some 11 years, "The Clark Kent and Superman Saga" continues even today. *Clark Joseph Kent is a fictional

23

character appearing in American comic books published by DC Comics. His character has become ingrained in popular culture as a recognized iconic symbol. Clark Kent has become synonymous with secret identities and innocuous fronts, alter egos for ulterior motives and activities. His genius is that Clark Kent adopted a largely passive and introverted personality with conservative mannerisms. His voice is altered to a higher-pitched one, and a slight slouch to cast contrast to his strong and sure Superman identity. Well, his Superman persona is vastly opposite of his meek and mild Clark Kent character. *Superman is faster than a speeding bullet! More powerful than a locomotive! Able to leap tall buildings at a single bound! You know Superman…. "Look! Up in the sky! It's a bird! It's a plane! No… It's Superman! He defeats most of, if not all his foes, restoring justice, and providing a sense of safety. You know Superman, don't you?

The stark reality is that both, Clark Kent and Superman were always present, but one was suppressed in order for the other to manifest. *Clark Kent with a strong sense of purpose, morality, and compassion. Superman was raised to believe that his abilities are gifts not to be abused. In many ways Our Horizontal Relationships with Others is held hostage when the Vertical Relationship with God is suppressed. As men, we lack the power to overcome what has crippled us as long as we become comfortable with our alter-ego. We suppress quality time with our spouses, children, family and friends for a few moments to play hero to people who really never mattered much. We mask our real emotions because we are afraid of the critique from others who see us for who we really are. So then, our Clark Kent becomes the nemesis to our Superman or vice versa. We become weak in the areas we should have strength.

Our focus is misplaced because we enjoy the temporary moments of fantasized heroics.

One of my mentors made a profound statement to me during a very climatic time in my life. He said that, *"When your persona gets bigger than your person, then who you have become will kill who you are."* The profundity of that statement stares at me whenever I am tempted to grab my "Superman suit" when life is calling me to be "Clark Kent." The dilemma of a broken Horizontal Relationship with Others will fester in so many areas of your life.

1. **The Lack of Authentic Mentorship-** *There is a need for a major African-American male youth retreat and mentoring where young African-American males can be provided with the substantial information providing validity that can help them understand what they are facing. Looking in retrospect, African-American ancestors stood in the gap for their future generations by fighting against slavery, police brutality, racism, injustices and many more problems that the African-American community had to deal with during different eras in the United States.*

2. **The Lack of True Transparency-** *African-American youth fall victim to a multitude of problems and this message should serve as a serious wake up call for the entire African-American community. For example, Chicago experienced **508 homicides** and **over 1,800 shootings** in 2012. Over **80 percent** of the homicide victims were African-American. Men of color also make up **60 percent** of the prison population throughout the United States. This is not a good situation for African-American males considering the many problems African-American people had to endure here in the United States.*

*Everyone talks about solutions to crime and other issues plaguing the African-American male population, but the question remains are we paying any attention to the vast majority of African-American males who are being challenged in almost every category of survival,*

*Where is the transparency?*

**3. The Lack of Qualitative Interaction-** *There are several African-American males finishing college and leading very productive lives in the United States. However, the numbers reflect why the leaders in the United States should take a serious look at trying to help young African-American males deal with society and overcome adversity without falling victim to the many ills of society.*

**\*Dr. Cornel West** served as my professor and became a friend during my studies at Union Theological Seminary in New York City, made this statement in his book- **Race Matters:**

*"We have to recognize that there cannot be relationships unless there is commitment, unless there is loyalty, unless there is love, patience, persistence."*

Are you balanced in both areas? Remember, one directly affects the other substantially.

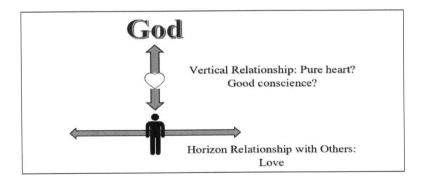

# Chapter 3

# Educational Attainment of African American Males: The Crisis of a Failed Educational System

*Chance W. Lewis, Ph.D.*

In a nation with the greatest resources in the world and a Gross Domestic Product (GDP) well-above other industrialized nations, a very disturbing trend is occurring as it relates to the African American male. In the area of education, the United States of America has some of the most prestigious universities in the world and has shaped the way we educate children to become productive citizens in society. However, right in the backyards of these great universities are various K-12 public school systems in this country that have failed many of the students that count on these same educational systems for social mobility. Over the past two decades, this has been especially true for the African American male. Noted author-scholar, Jawanza Kunjufu (2001), notes that as it concerns the African American male in our society, we are in a state of emergency.

Over the past decade, African American males have received a great deal of attention from the academic research community (Jackson & Moore, 2006; 2008; Polite & Davis, 1999) and the mainstream media about their academic shortcomings in American society, specifically detailing their educational attainment issues in our nation's K-12 schools. As an example, in 2006, the *Washington Post* ran a series of articles related to the plight of African American men and their presence in American society. However, as I have attempted to read, conceptualize and analyze all of this information, one thing I have clearly understood is that the nation's educational system has clearly failed the African American male. Being a former high school teacher and now a Distinguished Professor of Urban Education in the College of Education at one of the nation's premier universities (University of North Carolina at Charlotte), it truly breaks my heart because many educators, not all, have simply written off a population of students, which in most cases is the African American male.

In serving as a consultant to many school districts across the United States, I am utterly shocked at the many excuses educators give for the lack of achievement of African American males. Some of these educators detail their home lives as the main reason for the lack of educational attainment. Others detail the lack of parental support. Another group details their behavior at school. The issues go on and on depending on where I visit across the country. While some of these issues are valid, this does not mean that the African American male is uneducable and cannot achieve (Jackson & Moore, 2006). Truth be told, the authors of this book would not be where we are today if it were not for four main things: (1) the grace of God; (2) strong mothers; (3) a minimum of one strong male mentor; and (4) a committed educator who took the time to make a difference in our lives.

Nevertheless, as I develop my thoughts in this chapter, the main issue is the educational attainment of the African American male. Recent research (Children's Defense Fund, 2007; 2019) has documented that as it relates to the African American male, our nation's public schools are feeding one of two pipelines. One is the Cradle-to-College pipeline and the other is the Cradle-to-Prison pipeline.

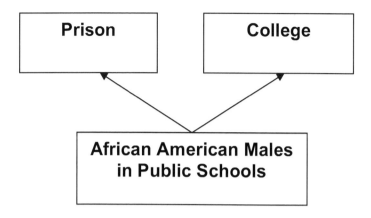

*Figure 1: African American Males and the Cradle-to-Prison and Cradle-to-College Pipeline*

In the Cradle-to-College pipeline, the African American male is groomed early in his life that college is a critical destination in his life. He is constantly reminded and provided the necessary resources by parents, community members, religious communities, schools and many others to move him along what educators refer to as the educational pipeline (Jackson, 2007). Fortunately, this African American male has all the necessary ingredients to lead a productive life.

Focusing on the Cradle-to-Prison pipeline, the African American male early in life may have a family structure that is filled with all types of problems. Unfortunately, in this situation, oftentimes, expectations for his life are never discussed or no one may have a vision of what he can do with his life. All the necessary ingredients that are needed for success (supportive parents, community members, religious communities, and educators who care) may not be available to this African American male at the same rate as the African American male mentioned earlier. Given this, the African American male feeds into what is called the

Cradle-to-Prison pipeline because of some of the things that are going on in his life. In looking at my own situation, the one factor that stands out is that educators (teachers, counselors, principals, etc.) who are paid to make a difference in the lives of these students often mis-educate their students and then force them to leave public schools either by graduation or voluntarily dropping out with a skill set that will at best give them a very low-paying job. This failure of our nation's educational system must be addressed if we are going to make change.

To help the reader understand the magnitude of this issue, let's examine the current state of African American achievement in comparison to their counterparts of other races in our nation's educational system.

### *Mathematics*

Table 4

*National Assessment of Educational Progress-Mathematics Grade 4 (In Percent)*

| Race | Below Basic | At Basic | At Proficient | At Advanced |
|---|---|---|---|---|
| African American | 37 | 44 | 17 | 2 |
| White | 12 | 37 | 40 | 11 |
| Asian American | 10 | 26 | 40 | 24 |

Source: National Assessment of Educational Progress (2019)

As we review the data presented in Table 4, it is clear to understand that African Americans clearly have an entirely different schooling experience, especially as it relates to academic achievement on standardized tests. In Grade 4, in the content area of Mathematics, we see that 81 percent (37 percent-Below Basic + 44 percent-At Basic) have not reached the "At Proficient" status. Stated differently, only 19 percent of African American 4th graders in Mathematics are 'proficient' in this content area.

Table 5

*National Assessment of Educational Progress-Mathematics Grade 8 (In Percent)*

| Race | Below Basic | At Basic | At Proficient | At Advanced |
|---|---|---|---|---|
| African American | 54 | 34 | 11 | 2 |
| White | 20 | 37 | 30 | 13 |
| Asian American | 14 | 25 | 31 | 30 |

Source: National Assessment of Educational Progress (2019)

According to Table 5, as African Americans move through the educational pipeline, their achievement patterns do not improve, in fact, they decline even further. As we see in this table, 88 percent (54% Below Basic + 37% At Basic) are still not proficient in Mathematics at Grade 8. We have to understand that these dismal numbers have larger social ramifications for these students. However, in the academic setting, it is clear that at least two main factors are occurring in the area of Mathematics: (1) African American students are not achieving; and (2) Educators are not preparing these students with the necessary skills to be successful in this content area.

### Reading

In the content area of Reading, which is another critical subject, the story for African American students, particularly African American males, does not change

31

much at all. Unfortunately, when African American students, males in particular, do not become proficient in Reading, their plight in society is greatly impacted. Let's review the data for Grade 4 in the content area of Reading.

Table 6

*National Assessment of Educational Progress-Reading Grade 4 (In Percent)*

| Race | Below Basic | At Basic | At Proficient | At Advanced |
|---|---|---|---|---|
| African American | 50 | 31 | 16 | 3 |
| White | 22 | 32 | 34 | 12 |
| Asian American | 18 | 25 | 35 | 21 |

Source: National Assessment of Educational Progress (2019)

Once again, we see the disturbing trend as it relates to African American achievement in Reading. According to Table 6, in 2019, 81 percent of African American students have not reached the "At Proficient" status at Grade 4. At this early stage of life, too many African American students are struggling to become proficient in Reading. What is happening in our schools in Reading?

Finally, in Grade 8, in the content area of Reading, let us examine the current trend of African American achievement.

Table 7

*National Assessment of Educational Progress-Reading*
*Grade 8 (In Percent)*

| Race | Below Basic | At Basic | At Proficient | At Advanced |
|---|---|---|---|---|
| African American | 41 | 42 | 16 | 1 |
| White | 17 | 40 | 39 | 5 |
| Asian American | 15 | 31 | 43 | 11 |

Source: National Assessment of Educational Progress (2007)

According to Table 7, we find that 83 percent of African American students have not reached the "At Proficient" status in the content area of Reading. Also, for the first time in our analysis of this data from the National Assessment of Educational Progress, we find that in the "At Advanced" category in Grade 8, there were only 1% of African American students at this level.

Conclusion

In sum, this chapter has provided a brief snapshot of the educational attainment of African American students, more specifically African American males. When we examine these data, we clearly see the ramifications of a failed educational system. However, we must ask the right questions to improve the educational plight of these students. Here are a few questions for us to consider as we look at the educational dilemmas facing African American students, particularly African American males:

- What educational reform efforts need to happen to turn the academic tide for the African American male?

- What can be done to improve academic achievement in these two critical content areas?

- What role should parents/community members play in this process?

- Why do schools continue to operate in a 'business-as-usual' mindset when children are failing at very high levels?

- What role should African Americans who have 'made it' give to African American students who are still in the educational pipeline?

These are just a few of the myriad of questions that need to be answered if we are all going to work together to solve some of the educational dilemmas that African American students, particularly African American males face in our K-12 educational institutions.

## References

Children's Defense Fund. (2007; 2019). Cradle-to-prison pipeline initiative. Available at http://cdf.convio.net/site/PageServer?pagename=Programs _Cradle

Jackson, J. (Ed.). (2007). Strengthening the African American educational pipeline. Albany, NY: State University of New York Press.

Jackson, J. & Moore, J. (Eds.). (2008). Beyond Brown: New approaches to addressing inequities in education for African American males. *American Behavioral Scientist, 51*(7).

Jackson, J. & Moore, J. (Eds.). (2006). African American males in education. *Teachers College Record, 108*(2).

Kunjufu, J. (2001). *State of emergency: We must save African American males.* Chicago, IL: African American Images.

Polite, V. & Davis, J. (1999). *African American males in school and society: Practices and policies for effective education.* New York: Teachers College Press.

U.S. Department of Education, Institute of Educational Sciences, National Center for Education Statistics (2007). *National Assessment of Educational Progress, 2007 Trial Urban District Assessments—Math and Reading.* Washington, DC: Author.

*"The only justification for ever looking down on*

*somebody is to pick them up."*

**Rev. Jesse Jackson**

Chapter 4

# The Dilemmas of Unemployment and Underemployment for African American Males

*Chance W. Lewis, Ph.D.*

"When American gets sick, the African American
community catches pneumonia"
*-Author Unknown*

A t the time of writing this chapter, one major *dilemma* or question that is facing the American society as posed by several economists is as follows: "Is the United States in a recession?" Many economists note that when looking at all the symptoms, it seems as if we are in a recession but no one really has the guts to call it what it is. No matter what we call this issue or how we look at this issue, the fact remains that the African American community will suffer a greater impact than most other communities in this country. This is not to say that a recession does not impact everyone but the famous quote by an unknown author states that "when America catches a cold, the African American community catches pneumonia" is quite evident.

To be even clearer to the readers of this book, even before this "recession" in the American society, the African American male continues to face another *dilemma*, which are unemployment and underemployment issues. By facing these types of *dilemmas*, it puts the African American male in an awkward position, that really no man wants to be in, wondering if he can provide financially for himself and his family. It is amazing that when unemployment rates are reported on television, they are only reported in general terms. However, when we take an in-depth examination into this data (to be reported later in this chapter), we find that the unemployment rates are much higher in the African American community, especially for African American males. Notwithstanding, is another issue that does not get the same type of media attention, is the underemployment issues of African American males. As a result of these two distinctive, yet intertwined *dilemmas*, this chapter will further elaborate on how these issues impact the African American male. Further elaborating on how various systems work in this society, this chapter will also explore how unemployment and underemployment play out in other areas of life for African American males.

***Unemployment Issues for African American Males***

To set the stage for this chapter, I am using the following definition for unemployment: "a person who is able to work but cannot find work or has been laid off from work and has not found other employment." Given this definition, there are many African American males who have the ability to work but are unable to find work or have been laid off from their jobs. So, we must examine if this *dilemma* is a heavier burden for the African American male than their White male counterparts.

Table 8
*Unemployment Rates—African Americans and Whites*

| Category | African Americans | White Americans |
|---|---|---|
| Unemployment Rate (Male & Female) | 7.5% | 3.8% |
| Unemployment Rate (Male Only) | 8.1% | 3.8% |

Source: National Urban League (2018)

38

According to the data in Table 8, the unemployment rates for African Americans are more than double that of their White counterparts. For African American males and females, the unemployment rate is 7.5% in comparison to 3.8% for their White male and female counterparts. Focusing specifically on African American males, we find that 8.1% of African American males are unemployed in comparison to only 3.8% of White males.

To the common eye, it is quite easy to see that this is more than double the percentage of White males. However, we must look deeper inside the numbers to measure the impact of this. We must understand that there are less African American in the United States than White Americans. Data has documented that there are approximately 36,121,000 African Americans in this country with 16,794,000 being African American males (U.S. Census, 2004).

Table 9

*African Americans in the United States*

| Category | African Americans (Male and Female) | African Americans (Male Only) |
|---|---|---|
| Total Population in the U.S. | 36,121,000 | 16,794,000 |

Source: U.S. Census Bureau (2019)

As a result, when we look at the numbers of 7.5% or 8.1% of African Americans, in particular African American males being unemployed is far more detrimental to the African American community than the White community. These percentages silently tear away at the fabric of African American communities because the African American male is unemployed at greater rates than other

39

ethnic groups. Unfortunately, when this large of a percentage of men are unemployed, a variety of other social ills (which are too many to discuss in this chapter) are attributed directly to unemployment. Also, the reader should clearly understand that this data does not factor in the number of African American males that are incarcerated that are also not financially contributing to the needs of their families and others within the African American community. To summarize this section, the African American male is definitely facing a *DILEMMA* in the area of unemployment.

### *Underemployment Issues for African American Males*

As I continue to explore the issues or *dilemmas* facing the African American male, as previously stated, unemployment is definitely an issue but another issue that does not get the widespread publicity is the notion of underemployment for the African American male. There may be a variety of reasons why underemployment is not widely reported. From a research perspective, it is not as easy to find reliable data that focuses in on underemployment. However, in my quest to bring to the forefront the *dilemmas* African American males face on a daily basis, Table 9 illustrates the ripple effects of underemployment.

First, I will report on how African Americans (males and females) are paid less than their White male counterparts. Second, in Table 10, I document the disparity in pay between African American males and White males.

Table 9

Median Household Income in 2018 by Race

| Category | African Americans | White Americans |
|---|---|---|
| Median Household Income | $38,555 | $63,155 |

Source: National Urban League (2018)

According to Table 3, this data illustrates that in 2018, African Americans (male and female) median household income was $38,555 in comparison to $63,155. As the data illustrates, there is approximately a $25,000 difference in income between African American and White households.

Table 10

Median Male Earnings by Race

| Category | African Americans | White Americans |
|---|---|---|
| Median Household Income | $39,431 | $43,346 |

Source: National Urban League (2018)

Table 4 illustrates that African American males earn a median income of $39,431 in comparison to $43,346 for White males (National Urban League, 2018). As I mentioned earlier in this chapter, from a data reporting standpoint, it is not easy to get data related to underemployment; however, when we examine the data above, we see the ripple effects of underemployment with the median male earnings. Unfortunately, for the African American male, the *dilemmas* continue. While this data does not provide information on the educational background of those in the sample or years of experience on the job, it does provide evidence that many African

American males are not paid at the same level as their White counterparts.

## CONCLUSION

In writing this chapter, as an African American male, I must say that this was quite troubling visualizing in my mind all of the ripple effects of African American males being unemployed and underemployed. In the solutions section of this book, I will address some potential solutions to these issues. Also, in the next chapter on economic issues, I will also elaborate on some of the ripple effects of the disparity in income for the African American male as a result of unemployment and underemployment issues. It is my prayer that someday every African American male that is able to work, will find gainful employment and be able to earn a competitive wage on the same level or even better than their White male counterparts.

## References

National Urban League. (2018). *The state of Black America 2018.* New York: Author.

U.S. Census Bureau. (2019). *Demographics of the United States.* Washington, DC: Author.

Chapter 5

# The Dilemmas of Substance Abuse for African American Males

"Let us not forget who we are. **Drug abuse** is a repudiation of everything America is."
President Ronald Reagan

*Kris F. Erskine, Th.D.*

The words of former President Regan haunt the very streets and neighborhoods of inner cities and rural communities across America. Substance abuse is now being seen in pandemic proportions. The NCJRS (National Criminal Justice Reference Service) website reported that an estimated 12.8 million Americans, approximately 6 percent of the household population ages twelve and older, use illegal drugs on a current basis (within the past thirty days). This number of "past-month" drug users has declined by almost 50 percent from the 1979 high of twenty-five million -- a decrease that represents an extraordinary change in behavior. Despite the dramatic drop, more than a third of all Americans twelve and older have tried an illicit drug. Ninety percent of those who have experimented with illegal drugs used marijuana or hashish. Approximately one-third used cocaine or took a prescription type drug for non-medical reasons. Other estimates document that one-fifth used LSD. Fortunately, nearly sixty million Americans who used illicit drugs during youth, reject these substances as adults.

Many people do not understand why individuals become addicted to drugs or how drugs change the brain to foster compulsive drug abuse. They mistakenly view drug abuse and addiction as strictly a social problem and may characterize those who take drugs as morally weak. One very common belief is that drug abusers should be able to just stop taking drugs if they are only willing to change their behavior. What people often underestimate is the complexity of drug addiction—that it is a disease that impacts the brain and because of that, stopping drug abuse is not simply a matter of willpower. Through scientific advances, we now know much more about how exactly drugs work in the brain, and we also know that drug addiction can be successfully treated to help people stop abusing drugs and resume their productive lives. It challenges us to research "What is drug addiction?"

### *What is drug addiction?*

Drug addiction is a chronic, often relapsing brain disease that causes compulsive drug seeking and use despite harmful consequences to the individual that is addicted and to those around them. Drug addiction is a *brain disease* because the abuse of drugs leads to changes in the structure and function of the brain. Although it is true that for most people, the initial decision to take drugs is voluntary, over time, the changes in the brain caused by repeated drug abuse can affect a person's self-control and ability to make sound decisions, and at the same time send intense impulses to take drugs. It is because of these changes in the brain that it is so challenging for a person who is addicted to stop abusing drugs. Fortunately, there are treatments that help people to counteract addiction's powerful disruptive effects and regain control. Research shows that combining addiction treatment medications, if available, with behavioral therapy is the best way to ensure success for most patients.

Treatment approaches that are tailored to each patient's drug abuse patterns and any co-occurring medical, psychiatric, and social problems can lead to sustained recovery and a life without drug abuse.

Similar to other *chronic, relapsing* diseases (diabetes, asthma, and heart disease), drug addiction can be managed successfully. And, as with other chronic diseases, it is not uncommon for a person to relapse and begin abusing drugs again. Relapse, however, does not signal failure—rather, it indicates that treatment should be reinstated, adjusted, or that alternate treatment is needed to help the individual regain control and recover.

### What happens to your brain when you take drugs?

Drugs are chemicals that tap into the brain's communication system and disrupt the way nerve cells normally send, receive, and process information. There are at least two ways that drugs are able to do this: (1) by imitating the brain's natural chemical messengers, and/or (2) by over stimulating the "reward circuit" of the brain. Some drugs, such as marijuana and heroin, have a similar structure to chemical messengers, called neurotransmitters, which are naturally produced by the brain. Because of this similarity, these drugs are able to "fool" the brain's receptors and activate nerve cells to send abnormal messages.

Other drugs, such as cocaine or methamphetamine, can cause the nerve cells to release abnormally large amounts of natural neurotransmitters, or prevent the normal recycling of these brain chemicals, which is needed to shut off the signal between neurons. This disruption produces a greatly amplified message that ultimately disrupts normal communication patterns.

Nearly all drugs, directly or indirectly, target the brain's reward system by flooding the circuit with dopamine. Dopamine is a neurotransmitter present in regions of the brain that control movement, emotion, motivation, and feelings of pleasure. The over-stimulation of this system,

45

which normally responds to natural behaviors that are linked to survival (eating, spending time with loved ones, etc.), produces euphoric effects in response to the drugs. This reaction sets in motion a pattern that "teaches" people to repeat the behavior of abusing drugs. As a person continues to abuse drugs, the brain adapts to the overwhelming surges in dopamine by producing less dopamine or by reducing the number of dopamine receptors in the reward circuit. As a result, dopamine's impact on the reward circuit is lessened, reducing the abuser's ability to enjoy the drugs and the things that previously brought pleasure. This decrease compels those addicted to drugs to keep abusing drugs in order to attempt to bring their dopamine function back to normal. Additionally, they may now require larger amounts of the drug than they first did to achieve the dopamine high—an effect known as *tolerance*. Long-term abuse causes changes in other brain chemical systems and circuits as well. Glutamate is a neurotransmitter that influences the reward circuit and the ability to learn. When the optimal concentration of glutamate is altered by drug abuse, the brain attempts to compensate, which can impair cognitive function.

Drugs of abuse facilitate non-conscious (conditioned) learning, which leads the user to experience uncontrollable cravings when they see a place or person they associate with the drug experience, even when the drug itself is not available. Brain imaging studies of drug-addicted individuals show changes in areas of the brain that are critical to judgment, decision-making, learning and memory, and behavior control. Together, these changes can drive an abuser to seek out and take drugs compulsively despite adverse consequences—in other words, to become addicted to drugs. My research has provided me with shocking facts concerning "Why some people become addicted, while others do not.

## Why do some people become addicted, while others do not?

No single factor can predict whether or not a person will become addicted to drugs. Risk for addiction is influenced by a person's biology, social environment, and age or stage of development. The more risk factors an individual has, the greater the chance that taking drugs can lead to addiction. For example:

- **Biology.** The genes that people are born with—in combination with environmental influences—account for about half of their addiction vulnerability. Additionally, gender, ethnicity, and the presence of other mental disorders may influence risk for drug abuse and addiction.

- **Environment.** A person's environment includes many different influences—from family and friends to socioeconomic status and quality of life in general. Factors such as peer pressure, physical and sexual abuse, stress, and parental involvement can greatly influence the course of drug abuse and addiction in a person's life.

- **Development.** Genetic and environmental factors interact with critical developmental stages in a person's life to affect addiction vulnerability, and adolescents experience a double challenge. Although taking drugs at any age can lead to addiction, the earlier that drug use begins, the more likely it is to progress to more serious abuse. Given that adolescents' brains are still developing in the areas that govern decision-making, judgment, and self-control, they are especially prone to risk-taking behaviors, including trying drugs of abuse.

Today, substance abuse disorders continue to proliferate in alarming numbers, especially in the African-American community. African Americans comprise approximately 12% of the population in the United States, yet in 1999 they accounted for 23% of admissions to publicly funded substance abuse treatment facilities. Consequently, there is a great need for more culturally sensitive and efficacious treatment targeted to the special needs of this minority population. Substance abuse is different than that in other communities. Reports indicate that drugs and alcohol are targeted in the African American community on purpose.

The availability of substance abuse is higher in the African American community. The billboards promote this degrading lifestyle and become an accepted way of life for the citizens trapped in a war zone for survival. Although African Americans have made tremendous social and economic advances during the past several decades, the tradition of African Americans being viewed as a racial group-rather than a cultural group-continues to adversely affect their psychological well-being.

Until recently, white male populations have dominated studies of substance abuse, with little focus on gender, ethnicity and etiologic variations. These cultural biases and the emphasis on majority American values and lifestyles may contribute to the presence of substance abuse behaviors in the African American community. The quote by former President Reagan is typical of a society that is committed to looking in the other direction.

We have long viewed Substance Abuse as a problem, but seemingly now that the numbers of whites are increasing- we have developed a "war on drugs." **"Just Say No"** was a television advertising campaign, part of the US "War on Drugs" and prevalent during the 1980s and early 1990s, to discourage children from engaging in recreational drug use by offering various ways of saying *no*. Eventually, this also expanded the realm of "Just Say No" to violence, premarital sex, and any other supposed vices that young people might try. The slogan was created and championed by former First Lady Nancy Reagan during her husband's presidency.

To meet the treatment needs of the African American substance abuser in a culturally sensitive manner, care providers must understand the variables that interface with the disorder. There are a number of variables related to socio-cultural factors in substance abuse. Research designs on substance abuse often do not address descriptive variables such as gender, age, income/wealth, geographic locations and cultural patterns. These variables play an essential role in differentiating drug-use patterns, whether between ethno-racial groups or within them. To properly assist the addicted, we must tell them more than just say no. We must have something for them to say yes to! Many have no formal education and it limits their potential for employment. Crippled by unemployment and/or under-employment-which is worst in many cases-and a growing substance abuse problem many African American men have loss a sense of hope.

In the African American community, crime is an offspring to an addiction to Substance Abuse. A 1992 study identified poverty, illiteracy, limited job opportunities, poor education, high availability of drugs, and stresses of the urban lifestyle as underpinnings of substance abuse in the black community.[4] Other researchers have found that environmental factors, such as the large number of liquor stores in African American communities, influence the heavy use of alcohol among black Americans.[5]

In addition, many African Americans have been subjected to violence as a primary oppressor, which robs the community of the resources needed to solve drug problems. Violence does not only present in the form of crime or domestic disputes but also in the context of racial discrimination, lack of access to food and clothing, homelessness, overcrowded living conditions, lack of health insurance, and restricted social welfare policy. African American women have experienced other forms of violence, such as sexual harassment, gender discrimination, and a lack of protection from domestic violence. Thus, the decline of the African American family unit and its unity!

## 2nd Addition Reflections

The privilege to speak to some 1700 inmates at Donaldson West Jefferson Correctional Facility here in Alabama is a sheer delight. The Chaplain, Rev. George Adams, has afforded me the opportunity to minister and mentor many of these men. Their attendance is not mandatory, but I am always battling emotions when I enter at a minimum of 3 times a year. There is the familiarity of faces over the past 4 years that is frightening to know that some of these men will die here. The opposing emotions are the new faces, younger and younger each visit. Their tattered testimonies are somehow intertwined with Substance Abuse. The Center for Prisoner Health and Human Rights-Incarceration, Substance Abuse, and Addiction stated that:

*Approximately half of prison and jail inmates meet DSM-IV criteria for substance abuse or dependence, and significant percentages of state and federal prisoners committed the act they are incarcerated for while under the influence of drugs. Data from a national study in five major American cities shows that at the time of arrest,* **63% to 83%** *of arrestees had drugs in their system, with marijuana and cocaine being the most common.* **Between 2000 and 2013**, *the percentage of arrestees with opiates in their system increased, with a couple of cities seeing significant increases in opiate presence, as well as methamphetamines.*

*Substance abuse and addiction have other significant public health implications;* **CDC data estimates that 7.6% of new HIV diagnoses between 2008 and 2011 involved transmission via injection drug use, and sharing needles and other equipment used to inject drugs is the most common form of Hepatitis C transmission.** *Substance abuse may be compounded by co-occurring mental illness, and many begin to use substances to cope with mental illness or physical pain.*

Because substance abuse has many similar root connections as other mental health disorders and illnesses, there is often a strong connection between mental illness and addiction. Newer research is defining mental illness as a brain disorder as maladaptive brain functioning is often responsible for mental disorders. While visiting "The Legacy Museum: From Enslavement to Mass Incarceration and The National Memorial for Peace and Justice in the month of March 2019, my wife and children made some startling discoveries. The systemic pipeline from slavery to mass incarceration is paved with African American males who were the victims of abuse overtly and covertly.

The vivid pictures, videos and tapped testimonies of men snatched from their families and communities has left an undeniable tear in the fabric of our society as African Americans. The prevalent Substance Abuse problem that is escalating daily is seemingly gone unaddressed. As a matter of fact, it is being used to substantiate injustices with men of color. This fact is supported by a recent *Washington Post article- "Undoing unjust prison sentences in Maryland, One Case at a Time"- by Todd Oppenheim on March 9, 2018… Todd Oppenheim is a lawyer in the felony trial division of the Baltimore City Public Defender's office.

*"Getting a 25-year prison sentence without parole for a drug conviction nearly crushed 37-year-old Tracey Vincent's hopes of changing his life. He later discovered that his cellmate was serving less time for a violent offense, it was like pouring salt on an open wound. Vincent grew up in East Baltimore and started selling drugs at the age of 13, with the encouragement of his father. Almost as soon as he started dealing drugs, Vincent, just like so many others, started using them.*

Mr. Oppenheim stated in the article: *"Luckily for my client, Maryland passed the **Justice Reinvestment Act** in 2016. **Justice Reinvestment** is a **national movement** calling for reductions in sentencing for many nonviolent offenses to reduce incarceration. Maryland's law reduced penalties for drug possessions and theft crimes, and it lessened the sting from minor probation infractions. It is also eliminated mandatory-minimum sentencing in drug cases. The state legislature provided one year- **October 1, 2017, through September 30, 2018**- to ask for reconsideration of past mandatory sentences. Todd Oppenheim's office is handling about 40 requests for Baltimore alone."*

"On January 12, 2019, Vincent and Todd Oppenheim stood in the same courtroom where, six years before, he had thought his life was virtually over. Mr. Oppenheim shared Vincent's story with the judge. He introduced his social worker and a release plan that included drug treatment and follow-up. Vincent's family was there. Despite the State of Maryland's objection to immediate action, the judge showed compassion and understanding and agreed to release Vincent on probation."

In conclusion, the article ended with Mr. Todd Oppenheim revealing: "Undoing Vincent's sentence is a momentary victory, but it is a drop in the bucket in the push for justice reinvestment."

In the first addition of Dilemmas of Being AA Male, I chose to spotlight the issues and ill effects that substance abuse has on the community of color. The startling reality is that many of the men, just like the ones in Donaldson West Jefferson Correctional Facility, and prisons across this country need the attention because of substance abuse.

BlackDemographics.com/CRIME provides a visual.

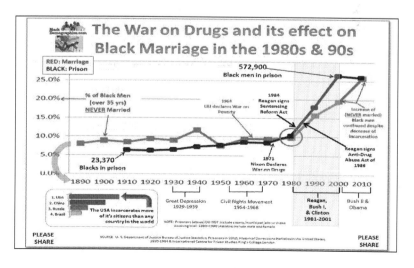

*"The battles that count aren't the ones for gold medals. The struggles within yourself-the invisible, inevitable battles inside all of us-that's where it's at."*

**-Jesse Owens**

# Chapter 6

## Economic Dilemmas Impacting African American Males

*Chance W. Lewis, Ph.D.*

At the time of writing this chapter, the major news headlines always have a focus on the status of the nation's economy. It seems that every report once to accurately predict if the nation's economy is favorable to economic prosperity. In the current headlines, reports surface that the nation's economy is strong and in a place where it has not been in recent years. Unfortunately, that economic prosperity does not hold true for African Americans, particularly African American males. A recent report from the United States Department of Agriculture documented that food prices (e.g., eggs, milk and other essential items) are at their highest prices in the past two decades. Notwithstanding, gas prices are just flat out ridiculous. In many areas of the U.S., the average price of gas is at or above $3 per gallon with the possibility of reaching $4 per gallon in the near future. Further, every evening on the local and national news, we hear another story about a major company or business that has decided to lay-off (downsize) thousands of workers in an effort to reduce costs. Even more disturbing is the fact that the foreclosure rates on homes are occurring at such a rate that it is even hard to calculate by economists. Too say it plainly; many Americans are in trouble financially. More specifically, African American males are facing some serious economic dilemmas that are impacting their daily lives. As a result, it is the goal of this chapter to clearly lay out a few of the economic *dilemmas* facing African American males so we can begin to discuss solutions to these issues later in this book. To fulfill these objectives, I utilize data from the National Urban League (2018) to paint a picture of the economic issues facing the African American male: (a) Mean Income Disparities; (b) Poverty; and (c) Housing and Wealth Formation.

## Mean Income

One cannot fully explore the economic *dilemmas* facing the African American male without an examination of the mean income of the African American male in comparison to his White male counterparts. I previously documented this data for you in the previous chapter on unemployment and underemployment (Chapter 4); however, I think it is important to show this data again as a foundation for this chapter.

Table 11

*Median Male Earnings by Race*

| Category | African Americans | White Americans |
|---|---|---|
| Median Household Income | $38,555 | $63,155 |

Source: National Urban League (2018)

As I mentioned earlier in this book, African American males have a large disparity in mean income in comparison with their White male counterparts of $25,000. Right at this point, we see the *dilemma* for African American males because when you make less, you are restricted with how much can do financially for your family, yourself and your community. Also, I want to illustrate that when African American males make less money, a cycle of other issues or *dilemmas* begins for this population.

## Home Ownership

To examine one strand of this cycle for the African American male, we must examine how many African American males own their own homes. This is a very important indicator of the economic well-being because "it is easier to secure a business loan if one owns a home and can use it as collateral, thus housing can directly contribute to wealth formation" (Thompson & Parker, 2007, p.19). Also, home ownership allows people to be more flexible in other types of financial matters. As a result, Table 2 documents two important items in homeownership rates for African American males: (1) African American and White male percentages that own a home; and (2) the median home values of the houses that they own.

Table 12

*Percentage of African American males and White males that own Homes and their Associated Values*

| Category | African American Males | White Males |
|---|---|---|
| Home Ownership % | 41.6 | 71.9 |
| Home Values | $103,239 | $147,433 |
| Equity in Home | $64,000 | $196,000 |

Source: National Urban League (2007)

In examining Table 12, we find that in the area of homeownership only 41.6% of African American males own their own home. For White males, 71.9% own a home. Given that less than 50% of African American male adults own their own home is a serious *dilemma*. Given that we have to live somewhere; oftentimes, we (African American males) are living in places that we have to rent (apartments, rent houses, etc.) and ultimately, we are not getting any

57

return on the money that is being paid out. We do not receive any tax breaks or other financial benefits of ownership. As a result, the African American male is left further behind on the economic barometer because of a smaller percentage owning their homes.

Another *dilemma* we can derive from Table 12 is that even when the African American male owns his own home, the value of that home is less than the value of a home of his White male counterpart. According to Table 12, the median price of a home that an African American male owns is $103,239 in comparison to $147,433 for his White male counterpart. I want to stress that this is important because the more that a home is worth, the more flexibility you have in using it as collateral to obtain more financial wealth. So, for African American males, the flexibility of using the equity in their homes for other financial endeavors is greatly reduced because they do not have as much equity to build more wealth. Table 2 illustrates that African American males have a median of $64,000 of equity in their homes compared to $196,000 for White males. So, this is a difference of $132,000 which greatly diminishes what African American males can do from the equity in their homes. This is a *dilemma*!

Another strand of the economic *dilemmas* that we must examine for African American males is their net worth. Basically, the formula for calculating net worth is (***assets [what you own] – liabilities [what you owe] = net worth).*** Given the previous information presented in this chapter, I think it is important to really examine the net worth of African American males in comparison to their White counterparts. As a result, Table 13 provides us with the most current financial information related to African American males in comparison to White males.

Table 13

*Net Worth*

| Category | African American Males | White Males |
|---|---|---|
| Net Worth | $13,229 | $118,000 |

Source: National Urban League (2018)

Table 3 documents for us that when examining net worth, African American males have a net worth of $13,229 in comparison to $118,000 net worth for White males. This difference of $115,000 poses a serious *dilemma* for the African American male because their 'financial standing' is not as strong as their White male counterparts. As a result, oftentimes, this leaves the African American male in a situation where they have plenty of debt and not much room to save funds or invest in their retirement, thus meaning they will have to work longer to survive financially. Thus, it is important to examine data on how many African American males are investing in their retirement accounts.

Table 14

*Investments in Retirement Accounts*

| Category | African American Males | White Males |
|---|---|---|
| % Investing in 401K | 33.6 | 60.4 |
| % investing in IRA | 13.2 | 46.5 |

Source. National Urban League (2018)

In examining Table 14, we find that African American males area far behind their White male counterparts in investing for their retirement. We find that only 33.6% of

African American males who are employed are actively investing in their company 401K retirement plans. This is in comparison to 60.4% of White males. Additionally, when examining the percentage of African American males investing in Individual Retirement Accounts (IRAs), we find only a meager 13.2% of African American males contributing to these investment vehicles in comparison to 46.5% of White males. Unfortunately, this data only provides us with a snapshot of the percentage of males (African American and White) who are participating in these retirement investments. What we cannot deduce from this table is how much (in dollars) are being saved by these two groups. As a result, this economic *dilemma* has impact on the lifespan of the African American male and impact on what is called "generational wealth" which I will explore in the next book in this series.

### Mortgage Application Denial and Home Improvement Loans

The last strand I want to focus on is the ability of the African American male to obtain a mortgage and then possibly pursue a Home Improvement loans on his property. This variable is very important because many think it is easy to obtain a home. However, if a person is not paying cash for a property they must obtain a mortgage. If they are successfully able to obtain a mortgage; oftentimes, many people seek to obtain a home improvement loan to improve the value of their home. As a result, Table 5 provides data on the mortgage denial and home improvement loan denial rates for African American males and White males.

Table 15

*Mortgage Application (Male) Denial Rates and Home*
*Improvement Loan Denial Rates (Male)*

| Category | African American Male | White Males |
|---|---|---|
| Mortgage Application Denial | 26.5% | 9.2% |
| Home Improvement Loan Denial | 55.9% | 27.4% |

Source: National Urban League (2018)

In Table 15, we see the great disparity in mortgage application denials. For African American males, approximately 26% of their applications are denied for a mortgage. This is in comparison to approximately 9% for White males. Given these numbers, plenty of conclusions can be drawn as to why these denials are occurring. However, we can understand that African American males do not have the same resources to purchase homes as their White male counterparts. Thus, without access, all of the data I presented in this chapter is affected.

Focusing on home improvement loans, we find that approximately 55.9% of African American males are denied in comparison to 27.4% for White males. These data are important to understand because this affects the ability of the African American male to improve the value of their home. As a result of the inability to enhance the values of their homes also greatly diminishes what the African American is able to do financially.

# CONCLUSION

This chapter has explored a myriad of issues that impact the African American male in the area of economics. I attempted to explore several items of importance: (a) median male earnings; (b) home ownership and home values; (c) net worth; (d) investments in retirement accounts; and (e) mortgage application denial/home improvement loan denial rates. While not inclusive of every economic indicator, this paints a picture of the economic *dilemmas* that African American males face on a daily basis. To get a more in-depth analysis, I would encourage you to read an excellent book entitled, *The Hidden Costs of Being African American* (Shapiro, 2004). Hopefully, after seeing the data in this chapter, some African American male somewhere will want to reverse these numbers and improve his financial standing.

## References

National Urban League. (2018). *The state of Black America 2007.* New York: Author.

Shapiro, T. (2004). *The hidden cost of being African American: How wealth perpetuates inequality.* New York: Oxford.

# The Solutions

*"I have learned over the years that when one's mind is made up, this diminishes fear; knowing what must be done does away with fear."*

*Rosa Parks*

# Chapter 7

# Repairing the Vertical Relationship with God

"No friends have I. I must live by myself alone; but I know well that God is nearer to me than others in my art, so I will walk fearlessly with Him." - Ludwig Van Beethoven

*Kris F. Erskine, Th.D.*

It is important to note that before something can be repaired there must first be an admission that it is not working properly. We have managed over the course of time to work with the non-functional. To basically get by with things the way they are and change when mandated. But change is inevitable and reception is better when initiated on our own terms. The responsibility factor must be constant if any profitable change is going to take place. Immediately after assessing this sensitive situation one would say to repair the vertical relationship with God there are some things you must do first. People would suggest to you just go to church or read the Bible, but I would have to disagree. There are many who attend church on a regular basis and have no relationship with God. Church attendance does not always equate a personal peace with joy and the spirit of love for God. These individuals lead double lives.

The character role they assume in public is quite different from the person they play in private. It is true-Who you are when you are alone always defines your character. The joy of jumping high in service and living life from a low state of depression will apply pressure of double jeopardy. Reading the Bible with no present disciplines with only promote confusion and frustration or sadly a judgmental attitude. Bible reading should be systematic and strategic as well as guided as a student of scripture so that answers can be supplied to each question. While church attendance is noble and Bible reading is rewarding there should first be a true examination of one's life. If we do not know where we are starting from, how will we know when we have arrived at our finish line? The ability to look within and ask the questions that have we have avoided is crucial to our survival and success. "How did I get here?" Where am I going? What is holding me from pursuing my dreams, goals and aspirations? What is the matter with me? Why is it so hard to focus? We must examine the dark horrid halls of our past and confront them with our relationship in God. I submit that we should assimilate into our vertical relationship with God via:

1) Prayer
2) Participation

The requirements of a rich a relationship with God is just like a recipe. It must be examined, studied and applied as the instructions suggest. Prayer is the ingredient that allows us to capitalize on the privilege God gives to all in relationship with him. It is the backbone of any vibrant vertical relationship-Communication. Jeff Herring wrote in an article on Relationship Advice-Keys to Communication that- **"Communication is the key in maintaining a connection with your partner."** Whoever we find ourselves communicating with the most will become the center of our attention.

To develop a relationship with God, prayer is the channel that allows open conversation with God. Now, communication is not just talking. There are no benefits in a relationship when one person does all the talking-monologue. However, God is seeking dialogue with us. Prayer, you may be asking, is followed by a myriad of questions.

Who can pray? Who is qualified and does God hear all prayers? When is the correct time to pray? When I pray will God answer? How will I know the answer is from God? Notice how the questions continue to compile on us. Anyone can pray. We must admit that most of the time we only execute this tool when we find ourselves in trouble or some calamity.

Prayer is great in our crucial moments when things are going crazy and in the opposite direction we desire. Prayer is great in our confusing moments when life seemingly robs us of our confidence and the stability we have come to rely on. But, prayer is also great when in our celebrating moments when things are well. The access of prayer to commune, communicate, and converse with God provides perpetual peace after the storms. It also provides directions when we cannot find our way. Prayer will give us the injection of assurance in our confidence that we all find ourselves needing from time to time. There really is no correct time to pray. In our world we are bombarded with appointments and schedules. The importance of scheduling and making appointments provides order to what would be a very hectic day. But, with God he does not need to pencil you or me in.

He is always available and desires to hear from you. He controls the hectic world we live in. You can develop a pattern in prayer, not prepared prayers, that will discipline you into a period of prayer. Daily communicating with God is the cleansing we need from day to day and from moment to moment. It will assist you in clearing our perspective on issues and seeing life from a better position. The power we experience from a consistent prayer life will define the voice of God in our ear. We will be able to discern and know the difference between what is God and what we are trying to make God. He will always answer your prayer. That is a promise-Jeremiah 33:3- "Call unto me and I will answer you and show you great and mighty things." He will not answer in the manner you want him to. However, He will always answer in the way you need Him to. This is a lifetime journey, take small steps and pray along the way! The more you pray, the more confidence you will develop and God will come alive in you! There is a church colloquium- "Little Prayer, Little Power; Much Prayer, Much Power; No prayer, No Power." I truly believe that where there is "Constant Prayer, there is Constant Power."

Prayer is the key to the kingdom of God, but faith unlocks the door. Prayer will, when people will not! After you position yourself in prayer, you then need to plan for participation. Participate in what you may be asking? In church attendance, ministry activities, outreach programs and mentoring opportunities. Antoine de Saint-Exupery once said, **"The notion of looking on at life has always been hateful to me. What am I if I am not a participant? In order to be, I must participate."** Getting involved will force you to prioritize your time. The "time factor" is important to the success of the Vertical Relationship with God. Idle time is filled with distractions that will keep us from achieving our goals and dreams. My mother would often tell me growing up that "an idle mind is the devil's workshop." Honestly, it was not until I had provided him an office in my mind and he was working full time with benefits before I realize the infection of idleness. Time is the only commodity of life that we cannot get any more of. We are getting older seemingly faster. The window of opportunity is beginning to close and for some sadly it already has. Time is crucial to the life as blood is to the body.

We must use our time wisely. The power of prayer will assist you in this, but participation will allow you to practice this. The problems with participating are:

1. Where should I Participate?

2. How should I Participate?

3. With what should I Participate?

Your *where* is a variable that will need to be carefully discovered. Do not rush. The sense of urgency will subside and the right choice will become evident. Your *where* will speak to your core values and beliefs and/or develop them for you. There is a passion connected to your participation that will come alive when you enter your *where*. Passion is important because it will be the driving factor when discouragement, *dilemmas* and disappointments arise. It will be the validation needed when times are well. I have often said that "passion is the fuel that makes your purpose move." The most successful people in the world are passionate about what they do. To convince someone that you enjoy doing whatever you do is obvious upon perception.

The lack of passion in participation is equivalent to a marriage with no love, parenting without direction, and smiling face with no joy in the heart. It is dangerous to commit to something or someone that you have no passion for. Participate in the areas where your strengths are magnified and your weaknesses are modified. Find areas where you can offer **you** and not just what you do. Second, there is How Should I Participate? Once you have settled on the *where* you will need to create a plan of action that will define your *how*. The *how* can never be accomplished until you have a sense of peace about your *where*. It is amazing that you do not tell fish to swim when they get in water, they just do it. They possess an innate ability to swim when they encounter their environment. Your environment will share with you the process to achieve your *how*. The environment will attract your *how*. As you produce your plan of action-What are the needs that I can assist with or meet? Where I am best utilized? What can be changed? What can only be altered? What is it that will never change?

These series of questions will enhance your plan of action. Never move into something without a plan. The Bible records in the Gospel of Luke 14:28- **"For which of you, desiring to build a tower, doesn't first sit down and count the cost, to see if he has enough to complete it?"** (World English Bible). The plans that fail are produced by those who fail to plan. Make sure what you offering is needed where you are offering it. You cannot give people what they "use to" need. How you get involved speaks strongly about your character. Are your aggressive or overbearing? Change should never be forced, but must be strategically positioned. I read a very interesting book "Who Moved My Cheese?" It gives different positions on the agent of change. Your past has determined a process of assessing that is seen in your day to day progression. John Stott, a theologian said, "Sow a thought, reap an action. Sow an action, reap a habit. Sow a habit, reap a character. Sow a character, reap a destiny." Last is the question of "With what I should Participate?" The feelings of inadequacy are often woven into the fabric of our lives without our knowledge. We do not feel as if what we do or who we are really matters from time to time.

The undeniable fact is that God has endowed us all with some unique qualities that are paramount in our purpose. You may be saying "not me" but yes you too. Your *"what"* is unmistakably your trademark! It sets you apart from everyone else. Dr. Seuss, author of the series of popular children's books once said, "Today **you** are **you** that is

70

truer than true. There is no one alive who is **youer** than **you**." As humorous as it may sound, the statement has tremendous validity to it. When God made you, he decided not to make (create and or develop) another you in the world! Your *what* is designed to assist you in reaching your destiny. Your *what* is the ingredient that sets you apart from the rest. Your *what* is the true you that you cannot mask and cover with the superfluities of life. No matter the clamor and clutter you have something valuable to offer in this life that is irreplaceable. Your *what* can easily be defined as your "It" Factor. Lao-Tzu: Inspirational Quotes: Ability- **"Knowing others is intelligence; knowing yourself is true wisdom. Mastering others is strength; mastering yourself is true power."**

These words, I truly believe are the frames for the "It" factor. It seems to be one of those nebulous, undefined, and subjective attributes one either has that cannot be explained with words. And it falls into the category of you-know-it-when-you-see-it. American Idol judge, Simon Cowell, periodically remarks about the "it" factor when assessing contestants. Some people call it passion. And while that's part of it, it goes beyond the intense driving focus associated with passion. I believe that it is rather PURPOSE. So, your *"what"* is your purpose. Whatever you are passionate about speaks directly to your purpose. The thing in life that you seemingly gravitate to is your purpose. But your *"what"* can always be discovered through your passion. I have often said that Passion is the fuel that makes ones Purpose move. Ask yourself right now; what am I really passionate about? Not generally associated with or things I just like or prefer. But what are those things you cannot see yourself not doing. That thing you feel the greatest sense of accomplishment from achieving. What is the underlying element that excites you like nothing else does? That is your "It" factor. That is the "What" of your life. This is where you should participate because without question that is what is needed in your *where* and *how.*

The feelings of low self-esteem are prevalent in the lives of those who may be offering their "what" in the wrong places. Be careful of this because people will exploit you while trying to rob you of your *what.* Your "*what*" is so priceless that you should discover what it is and guard it with all you have. The Bible records in the Gospel according to Matthew in chapter 16 and verse 26- "For what is a man profited, if he shall gain the whole world, and lose his own soul? Or shall a man give in exchange for his soul? The word "soul" here is a very interesting Greek word –psychue. Our English language has derived several words from its Greek root. Words like psyche, psycho and yes psychology, "the study of mind." The Bible implies here that in our journey through life our *where, how* and *what* are not worth bargaining with. The world will offer us some tempting things. We must be willing to say that our vertical relationship with God is far greater than any creature comfort we may find here.

## 2<sup>nd</sup> Edition Addition

In recent years, a number of Pew Research Center surveys have shown that Millennials in the United States – young adults born between 1981 and 1996 – are generally less religious than older Americans, based on our core measures of religious commitment. This holds true for black people, in that black Millennials tend to be less religious than older blacks. That said, black Millennials are considerably more religious than others in their generation, according to a new Pew Research Center analysis.

Black Millennials more religious than other Millennials, though less so than older black people. The article reported that about six-in-ten black Millennials (61%) say they pray at least daily, a significantly higher

72

share than the 39% of nonblack Millennials saying this. And while 38% of black Millennials say they attend religious services at least weekly, just a quarter (25%) of other Millennials do this, according to the analysis based on data from the Center's 2014 Religious Landscape Study.

In fact, nearly two-thirds (64%) of black Millennials are highly religious on a four-item scale of religious commitment – which includes belief in God and self-described importance of religion, in addition to prayer and worship attendance – compared with 39% of nonblack Millennials. At the same time, black Millennials are substantially less religious than older black adults by these measures. They are less likely than older black adults to say they pray at least daily, that they attend religious services at least weekly, and that religion is very important to them.

The Repairing of the Vertical Relationship with God seemingly is being created among those who receive the most criticism. The African American community is comprised with multi-generational representation.

*The Builders- are the individuals that was born approximately between 1922 and 1942. This generation is also known as "Traditionalists" and the "Silent Generation" because children of this ear were expected to be seen and not heard. The range in average age from 75 to 80 years old in 2018. Builders helped to establish the Vertical Relationship with God for the family. Heavy churched generation. Attended worship on a regular basis. In home devotions with prayer before meals. Very loyal to religious preferences. Change is antithetical to alignment. They developed a spiritual attitude and acumen from awkwardness of Slavery and Jim Crowism. The Builders and their parents were exposed to cruelty in highest form. The Repair of a Vertical Relationship with God was not only desired, but for the time in which they lived was

73

demanded. It was demanded for survival. Langston Hughes penned a poem entitled- "Mother to Son" that embodies the experiential need for this Vertical Relationship with God.

"Well, son, I'll tell you:
Life for me ain't been no crystal stair.
It's had tacks in it
And splinters
And boards torn up
And places with no carpet on the floor...
Bare.
But all the time
I'se been climbin' on,
And reaching landin's,
And turnin corners,
And sometimes goin' in the dark
Where there ain't been no light.
So boy, don't you turn back
Don't you set down on the steps
'Cause you find it kinda hard.
Don't you fall now-
For I'se still goin', honey,
And life for me ain't been no crystal stair."

**\*The Boomers**- are the individuals that were born between 1942 and 1962. This generation is characterized by the influence of strong traditional parenting, rules and regulations. This is the "Self-Willed" and "Liberal" generation. The Boomers Vertical Relationship with God has their foundation from their parental traditionalism. These individuals understood God by force, not by faith. It is why they are known for ushering in an era of protests that brought about transformative change in American society.

In a USC News article by Vincent Lim, he is quoted having said- "One of the things we found in our study of baby boomers — particularly among the older boomers — was that many are now more likely to be churchgoers or engage in spiritual practices than they did in their middle years," Bengtson said. "One in five of the 599 boomers in our study reported they had increased their religious or spiritual activities in recent years."

*The Busters- are the individuals that were born between 1963 and 1982. This group consists of those who are now approximately 30-50 years of age. This generation is characterized with mixed traditionalism and liberation theological values. Half of all Busters are from a single-parent home. Because the prioritizing of personal achievements for their parents was desire, the family structure and stability was lost. Thus as children born to Boomers, but raised and reared by Busters, have a keen sense of the Vertical Relationship with God bedrocks. The love and loyalty of their grandparents is hallmarked. Busters have a diverse perspective of church and the need for God's guidance. It is the love and loyalty to both Builders (Grandparents) and Boomers (Parents) that has this generation sometimes sinking in a proverbial quagmire. Due to the activism of their parents, Busters are highly influenced by community-orientation, service projects, and involvement.

So, it is apropos that the Repair of the Vertical Relationship would come from the most promising of all generations:

**The Bridgers**.
These individuals were born between 1983 and 2002. The world of Bridgers is multiracial and multicultural. Their economic world id divided between the "Haves" and the "Have Nots." They, like their parents, were raised by working mothers in single parent homes.

This generation is known as more confident than the Boomers. Many of the Bridgers have limited interaction with their grandparents (Boomers), and very myopic memory of their great-grand (parents (Builders). Their understanding of the Vertical Relationship with God is best shone in their need to have spiritual challenges. Unlike their predecessors, their spiritual hungry is satisfied not in a particular place, but a purpose. They need challenges biblically because they are eager to learn and put those values into practice with high expectations. Bridgers are very misunderstood by previous generations, but when studied they possess all the qualities of generations gone by.

The attitude of loyalty is a keen characteristic the Bridgers derived from their great-grandparents the Builders. Religiously, African Americans Millennials, are highest amongst those of different ethnicities. The research of their heritage solidifies the loyalty that was founded and fosters in a cultural they can connect with. One they must connect with. The Bridgers are so much like their Builder grandparents in that they possess that "selfless commitment" when directed to a calling higher than themselves. We have witnessed this in the Black Lives Matter Movement, the Me Too Movement, Occupy Wall Street, and a plethora of social movements that are selflessly committed. This is also attaching Bridgers to Boomers with a sense of activism. My research and relationship with Millennials have educated me that this generation is not comprised of those who "sit by and watch and pray." Bridgers, like their parents Busters, desire to have involvement in faith that fulfills. Repairing the Vertical Relationship with God is not just a Sunday morning experience, but a Monday through Saturday exercise.

Their parent's heart for community and development is shone here with projects I have assisted to develop for Bridgers entitled- RAKE Projects. RAKE is an acronym for Random Acts of Kindness Everywhere. Our hope for renewal and repair of the "Vertical Relationship with God" is a mixture of all those who have travelled before us, as well as those who will succeed us.

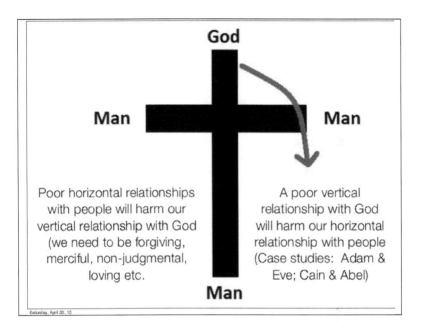

God

Man                    Man

Poor horizontal relationships        A poor vertical
with people will harm our         relationship with God
vertical relationship with God      will harm our horizontal
(we need to be forgiving,         relationship with people
merciful, non-judgmental,        (Case studies: Adam &
loving etc.                  Eve; Cain & Abel)

Man

Saturday, April 20, 13

*"Never be limited by other people's*

*imaginations."*

**Dr. Mae Jemison**

# Chapter 8

## Mending the Relationships with His Family

"Immature love says: I love you because I need you. Mature
love says: I need you because I love you."
Eric Fromm

*Kris F. Erskine, Th.D.*

It seems as if everyone is an expert on the subject of
relationships today. From the ever popular talk shows to
cinema screens, people need good advice about
relationships. I agree with Actress Gillian Anderson who
said, "Well, it seems to me that the best relationships – the
ones that last – are frequently the ones that are rooted in
friendship. You know, one day you look at the person and
you see something more than you did the night before. Like
a switch has been flickered somewhere. And the person
who was just a friend is…suddenly the only person you can
ever imagine yourself with." While we read in romance
novels how the two individuals fall madly in love
effortlessly and lived happy ever after, that is certainly not
the case with many of us. Relationships demand work!
And not only work but constant work.

As I explained in the chapter title "The Horizontal
Relationship with His Family," we are sometimes forced
into playing the role of Superman when actuality all we are
really is Clark Kent. The struggles of self identity and self
analysis cause many men to fear the reality of their lives,
"it scares us to death to face who we really are." The
inadequacies that we wear under our skin, and some on and
above it, have some men living in total chaos. We are
cumbered by so many activities that others assume we
should excel in. When we really have a hidden desire to
escape the pressures of life, we have allowed others to heap
upon us. We peep from under the shadow of the sudden,

79

hoping with every fleeting moment our Superman costume still fits. If we are going to mend the relationships we have with our families we must shake hands with our own reality. We must begin admitting to ourselves that there are some things that we just cannot accomplish. We either need the assistance of others and/or we need to admit that the thing has enveloped us and we are sinking hopelessly into an abyss of despair. It was Shakespeare in Hamlet that said:

*This above all:*

*To thine own self be true,*

*for it must follow as dost the night the day,*

*that canst not then be false to any man.*

I truly believe that is one of the secret gems of life that goes under appreciated and never realized. Before we can be anything productive, effective and even efficient to anyone else, it must first start within ourselves. How do you really see yourself? What is the greatest strength you have that you have hidden in the stereotypical ideologies of people? What goals do want to accomplish that you have shelved because of other commitments? Where on the map of your life are you really? I visited a mall and wanted to know where a particular store was located. At the entrance was a map of the mall. It listed every store with a correspondent alphabet next to it. I had to first read the list of stores to make sure the store I was looking for was even in the mall. After location the store, I had to notice the corresponding alphabet and remember it as I gazed over the map to find its location. When I finally located it on the map, a huge mall I might add, I immediately had to go back to the blinking star that read, **"YOU ARE HERE."** I could not find where I wanted to go until I understood where I was.

In life we proceed to find various locations of desire, pleasure, success, and security without first locating the sign, **"YOU ARE HERE."** Do not make another move until you discover where you are! Mending relationships also demand that you be honest. After facing your own areas of need, you qualify to assist others in theirs. As people, we are either introverted or extroverted. An Introvert as defined by Carol Bainbridge at About.com. "Contrary to what most people think, an introvert is not simply a person who is shy. In fact, being shy has little to do with being an introvert! Shyness has an element of apprehension, nervousness and anxiety, and while an introvert may also be shy, introversion itself is not shyness. Basically, an introvert is a person who is energized by being alone and whose energy is drained by being around other people." Is this you?

Now, the opposite of that is an Extrovert. The definition by Carol Bainbridge is: "Most people believe that an extrovert is a person who is friendly and outgoing. While that may be true, that is not the true meaning of extroversion. Basically, an extrovert is a person who is energized by being around other people. This is the opposite of an introvert who is energized by being alone." Is this you? I used these terms because most men fit securely into one or the other at specific times in our lives. A few Sunday's ago I was preparing for church, I watched a Pastor preach about the difference in men and women in relationships. He carefully explained this using metaphors that brought clarity to what is still a complex subject. The Pastor described men as waffles and women as spaghetti. Men, he explained, are liked waffles in that we have little boxes that we compartmentalize every scenario that we face. While explaining the little boxes, he added that we have placed dialogue in some and others that are empty on purpose to provide us areas of escape when life's issues stare us down. As men, we have the proclivity to avoid conversations openly that we are having privately. We process so different than our counterparts.

Women, on the other hand, he explained were like a plate of spaghetti. While on the same plate going in different directions seemingly with each noodle having its own agenda, still manages to connect with the others on the plate. Interestingly, women can multitask like no one else. The ability to fix dinner, while on the phone, and help kids with homework and sow buttons on her husband's favorite shirt comes somewhat easy to some of them. In mending the relationships with your family, be careful to omit the abilities and attributes that the woman in your life brings. This woman does not necessarily have to be your wife and/or significant other, she could be your mom, aunt and/or close friend. As a man, we can no longer afford to analyze the problems of life from just a male prospective. We could really provide restoration to our relationships if we would utilize all the resources surrounding. Do not be afraid to admit you cannot accomplish everything, but also you do not know everything. Honestly, when I developed the area of my character to be able to say to people, "I do not know," I began to walk in the spirit of freeness. When you admit this, on the surface it would seem you are weak and not well versed. But, I disagree. Others have said to me how much they appreciated my honesty and actually respected me more for it. Mending your relationships with your family is crucial. Admit to those you love the things you do not know when confronted with them and watch how the appreciation level for your honesty soars.

Another key component to mending your relationships with your family is the area of giving. Giving, you may ask, yes giving, but strategically. The biblical connotations of giving are based on the 3 T's.

**Time,**

**Talent**

**Treasure**

To mend your family, after assessing their needs, may reveal that your family requires more of your time. Time is an investment that we must be mindful of where we place it. It is the only commodity of life that we cannot get more of. Time is also precious as you master every moment you have to live. Small allotments of your time will go a long way in the mending process. Your family is screaming via rebellion, arguments for more of your time. Whether it is dropping the kid(s) off to school and/or picking them up to assisting with family chores. Seize every moment, small or great, to maximize your time with your family. Time cannot be replaced with money and materials. They do not want more things, the want more of you. To mend the relationships with your family with materialism is dangerous. You will promote the idea that your love can be purchased. Try reading a book to your children at bedtime. Cooking a meal with your spouse and watching a show that involves the entire family.

Second, give your Talent. Your talents are invaluable to the mending process. What you add to the family equation can never be replaced. The ideas that you possess and the dreams you have are connected to your talents. The area of expertise you have is like no one else. Share it! You could possibly have the cure for someone's crisis. Share it! The talents you have, others would need to go to school to learn but never perfect on the level you practice on. Share it! Your family is perishing because you have not shared what God has purposed you with. Talents come in a different range of areas. Define, then develop, what your talents are and use them wisely. Stop giving your talents away to those do not appreciate them. Your son needs them. Your daughter needs them. Your wife needs them. The time to reclaim your family is now. Do not allow another moment to pass without regaining your family. They are truly God's gift to you. Cherish them, and allow them to meet the part of you that has not been seen.

Last, you must give your treasure. The Bible records that a wise man leaves an inheritance for his children's children. Envision that, not just your children, but the children that your children will give birth to. The desire of every man should be to ensure the survival of his family at all cost. The remarkable thing about that scripture is that there will be people living off of what you provided who never met you personally. That is exciting to me. Because in death, I can add to the life of those I love. Your treasure may not altogether be finances. Your treasure could be your ideas and inventions and or insight. Allowing others to dig and find treasure in your field speaks greatly about your life's experience. The mistakes and miracles of your past should assist and aid others in their present.

The treasure you have could be you. Allow others to treasure you. I am blessed to have a Great-Grandmother who celebrated her 102nd birthday on March 23, 2008. I told her I would pay the price of patience for her wisdom. Just to be in her presence is priceless. I treasure her and the wealth of wisdom she leaks out in her conversation. Learn how to appreciate people for who they are and what they add to your life to make it better. Without them, you would never be all that you are and hope to become. So, mending the relationship with your family begins with you. Find the areas that you can improve and start doing it. You do not need to announce it, just do it.

You're doing will announce itself. Do not expect instant gratification. Setting yourself up for praise before you have proven yourself is dangerous. Remember, your reason for mending the family relationships is not about you, but the family. Take it slow. With your family members whose trust factor you have abused, take it slow. You have the remainder of your life to show them your sincerity. Do not pressure them to enter an area they are not comfortable with just yet. Mending takes time, but it is worth it!

## 2ⁿᵈ Edition Reflections

The major hurdle preventing men from mending the horizontal relationships in his life is summarized in word-ACCOUNTABILITY! This entire book has served as resource to provide transitional teaching. The books substratum is ACCOUNTABILITY. My goal in counseling and providing insight to men in relationships is that Assessment is followed closely by Accountability. The past 7 chapters have provided Assessment, now it is time for Accountability. Dr. Chance Lewis and I truly believe that empowering men is important to the survival of our culture and community. Black men voices matter as well. We have much to add to the conversation about our children and their decisions. Our voices matter. We have much to convey concerning the depravity of our communities and cities. Our voices matter. We are committed to communicating about the hopelessness that permeates all levels of education. Black men have immeasurable value and wealth of wisdom that is the catalyst for change.

There is another story about a young man I am eager to share with you. He was destined for greatness and success beckoned for him at a very early age. This young man was an heir to not only his father's throne, but also to succeed his grandfather. His blood was dripping with regality. He lived in the perfect surroundings with all of the accouchements.

Everything in life was set up for him. Until an unfortunate turn events happen one day. While his father and grandfather were off fighting in battle, the tragic news reached the kingdom of their fates. Both men died on the battle field defending their beloved country. The young man's moment of destiny seemed as if time sped up. At the age of 5 he is thrust into a destiny he is not prepared or ready for. In one day everything has changed. To make matters worse, the nurse in charge of attending to him, rushed to rescue him and dropped the young king. The custom of that time was whenever leadership changed, the new king would have the former king's family annihilated. This would eliminate the memory of the power from past. His nurse, unintentionally, dropped him and he landed on his feet crushing both of his ankles. A promising career shattered. Dreams and hopes dashed in seconds. The settings of this story would easily fit in the inner city of Chicago, New Orleans, Compton, Detroit, or even Birmingham. Young black men struck down by shots of senseless bullets.

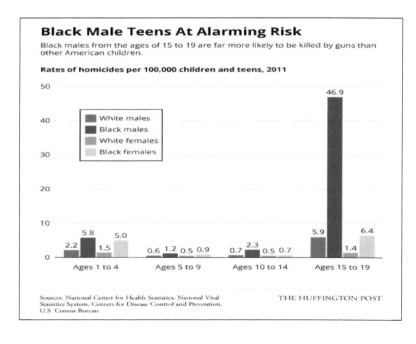

**Black Male Teens At Alarming Risk**

Black males from the ages of 15 to 19 are far more likely to be killed by guns than other American children.

**Rates of homicides per 100,000 children and teens, 2011**

Legend:
- White males
- Black males
- White females
- Black females

Ages 1 to 4: 2.2, 5.8, 1.5, 5.0
Ages 5 to 9: 0.6, 1.2, 0.5, 0.9
Ages 10 to 14: 0.7, 2.3, 0.5, 0.7
Ages 15 to 19: 5.9, 46.9, 1.4, 6.4

Sources: National Center for Health Statistics, National Vital Statistics System, Centers for Disease Control and Prevention, U.S. Census Bureau

THE HUFFINGTON POST

This is a sad commentary because the young man in our story was being held by hands that could not handle him. She dropped and injured his potential. He like so many men are the victims of being dropped by hands that could never handle what they were holding. The vast number of Ph.Ds. and lawyers, medical doctors, the next Zion Williamson basketball phenome, or Andrew Koonce-15, is a talented African-American violinist from Atlanta. Perhaps, Ginger Howard from Philadelphia, who is an American professional golfer on the Symetra Tour. At 17 she was the youngest African-American to turn professional and win her first debut tournament. This young man never arrived to his date with destiny because he was dropped. A lack of accountability. The nurse in the story serves as model and prototype to those in our communities of culture and color who improperly attempt to handle those whom we leave hurt. The "ACCOUTABILITY FACTOR" is the common thread in mending our Horizontal Relationships.

His life now, because of sensationalism, is swept from the front pages to a fading memory in the minds of the careless. This one day destined to be king, is living crippled. Too many men of culture and color never research the crippling they one day discover has them sidelined. Those who do, only stop there because of the payment pain to endure the exposure. This young man is living as do most men, with a crippling they did not cause. The sadistic attitude developed while living with our crippling is a sense of comfortability that negates healing. We have become comfortable with our crippling. As those the young man in our story. We find him leaving the grandeur of the palace to gruesomeness of pity- A place called Lodebar. It is proverbially "that place" where those who's potential has been punctured dwell. It is where high hopes and dreams go to die a slow and methodical death. Lodebar is a place where accountability is locked out and despair is the obstruction that prevents it entrance.

He is living in Lodebar. Despite all, he is the recipient of a covenant agreement between the new king and his dead father. The new king honors the covenant between him and friend and remembers the son he never knew existed. In mending the "Horizontal Relationships" accountability calls us to honor our covenants. We must again establish covenants within our communities. Covenants that are supportive and substantial to the survival of the next generations. Covenants such as the ones made during the days before slavery, and during the middle passage, and when slave ships docked, in the words of Maya Angelou-"these dis-United States." Covenants we created while picking cotton in the hot sun and beaten for assisting others to freedom. The new king remembers, and inquires and he sends for him out of Lodebar. The new king brings him, still crippled, to the palace that was once destined to be his. He brings him back to the place he belonged. The new king honors a covenant that this young man is not even aware of. He brings him back and tells him he will eat forever at the king's table. Now that is accountability.

1. What covenants have you created?
2. What covenants have you forgotten to honor?
3. Whose life has your impact made an impression?
4. How have you crippled the community or culture?
5. Who have you left behind for the cost of success?
6. Are you connected to the problem or the solution?
7. Are you ready to assume accountability?

# Chapter 9

## Improving Academic Achievement for the African American Male

*Chance W. Lewis, Ph.D.*

It is crystal clear that if the African American male is ever going to overcome some of the *dilemmas* he faces, educational attainment is critically important. In the chapter on the "Educational Attainment of African American Males," I provided the data that illustrates how African Americans, particularly African American males are at or near the bottom of every major academic barometer as it relates to academic achievement. We must understand that for African American males to greatly improve in the educational arena, a multi-faceted approach is necessary to make this happen. Further, we must understand that many people in this society do not want this group to improve as they continue to benefit financially off of their dismal performance in the academic ranks. Nevertheless, the goal of this book is to be life-changing. As a result, the purpose of this chapter is to explore solutions to assist African American males in the United States society to become productive citizens through educational attainment. Also, I seek to offer viable solutions on various levels that are especially important in improving the plight of African American males. So, I write this chapter in an unconventional way, with a heading of the general solution, with bullet points for emphasis, and a brief discussion of what needs to happen. I hope the words of this chapter encourage some African American male to realize the importance that education can have on his life.

*Solution #1: A Greater Emphasis on Education in the Home Environment*

Under Solution #1, I provide several key points that emphasize why education in the home environment will be critical for African American males to overcome some of the *dilemmas* that they face on a daily basis:

- *A Paradigm Shift Surrounding Educational Attainment must occur in the Home*

At this time in history, the African American male is on the verge of total extinction from society. However, we can change his plight as it relates to academic achievement simply by having a paradigm shift on how we view and approach education in the home environment. By this, I mean that the African American male should come to understand that it is the expectation that he does not just lie around the house and eat all of the food, watch television, and play video games; but he must be developing his academic skills on a daily basis. This must be planted in this spirit constantly so he can be reminded about the expectations for his life. As Kunjufu (2007) noted, the African American male should have posters put up in his room of the different colleges that he can possibly attend after high school. Kunjufu also noted that we (parents, community members, etc.) should clearly define what the expectations are verses some of the goals. For example, the African American male needs to know that the expectation is to graduate from high school AND FROM COLLEGE. That's the expectation. After meeting the expectations, he can then decide if he wants to reach the goal of obtaining a Master's or Doctorate degree.

So, I want this to be clear, we do not have to buy the young African American male a brand new car just because he graduates from high school because that is what he was expected to do. We must understand that education will be a *dilemma* that the African American male will face but we can prevent the impact of this *dilemma* by instituting a paradigm shift on how we view education in the home environment.

- ***Readers Become Leaders—The Home Environment must facilitate Reading as an Everyday Activity***

Some of you may have heard the population radio commercial that says, "Readers become Leaders." I firmly believe this statement. Reading is so important that I cannot stress it enough that African American males must learn how to read. There is a popular saying that says, "if you want to keep something from African Americans, just put it in a book." We have to change the mentality around reading in the African American community. As a result, here are some ideas of what should happen in the home to promote Reading:

1. At the Pre-Kindergarten age, African American males should be introduced to Reading through some type of reading program (e.g., (Hooked on Phonics, etc.);

2. Parents and/or caretakers of African American males should dedicate 1 hour for daily reading;

3. After reading, African American males should be able to summarize what they have learned;

4. African American males must develop their writing skills;

*Point #1*

At the pre-Kindergarten stage, it is especially important to introduce Reading to the African American male early because this is so critical to their success academically. Unfortunately, many of our young African American males enter Kindergarten not knowing how to read at all. This ultimately puts the African American male at a great disadvantage because the teacher who may have 25-30 other students in the class may not have the time to teach the fundamental skills of Reading to a child that is so far behind when he enters the classroom. So, I am suggesting that reading programs like Hooked on Phonics or any other program be introduced in the pre-kindergarten years. If the family does not have the financial resources to purchase these reading programs, they can be checked out from a local community library. Basically, the purpose of these literacy building programs is to develop a love for reading for all children. Further, these programs teach the fundamental skills needed for Reading such as Phonetics, Word Recognition, Pronunciation, etc. All of these skills are especially important for the young African American male to be able to understand if they are going to be adequately prepared to face all of the *dilemmas* that he will encounter in his schooling experience. We must remember, "Readers become Leaders."

*Point #2 – Dedication to 1 Hour of Daily Reading*

In order to have a paradigm shift in the home, I would encourage parents, guardians, grandparents or any other caretakers of African American males to dedicate 1 full hour of dedicated reading time for the African American male. I must warn you that the first time you implement this you will face resistance from him; however, I would encourage you to remain persistent because of the long-term benefits of this in his life. Depending on the age level, a variety of materials should be obtained from him to read. It doesn't necessarily matter what he is reading as long as it is something productive. This can be from pre-Kindergarten through adulthood. Truth be told, we need more men who are readers as well.

As many read this section of solutions, I understand that every family does not have the resources to buy a plethora of books that are available on a daily basis. However, this is why I want you to become really familiar with your community library. Once you obtain a library card, you can check these books out for free! All you have to do is turn them in on time and you will not have to pay any fines. Further, the reading does not just have to be books. The African American male also needs to read magazines and the daily newspaper to stimulate his intellectual development. We have to understand that with this daily exercise of reading, it will give birth to a hunger for more reading. However, parents and caretakers, we must remain persistent. Trust me; if we can get our young and older African American males to reading for at least 1 hour per day and cut off the television and video games, we will have new leaders emerging right before our very eyes. We must understand that when a book is put in front of these young men, you open up a world of new possibilities. I urge you to stay the course and encourage him to read because the knowledge he gains through reading may be the knowledge he needs to overcome future *dilemmas* in his life.

### Point #3—African American males need to summarize what they have read

Caretakers (parents, grandparents, etc.) as we continue in our discussion, we cannot just have the African American male take 1 hour and jut read in a room by himself. I am encouraging us to take it to the next level and require him to summarize his reading verbally. This is a critical important step for several reasons. First, you will know if he has truly completed his reading assignment. You have to do this because if he knows that he can get over without completing his reading he definitely will. Second, this will help him practice his verbal skills and public speaking skills. I would encourage all caretakers to have these African American males (of any age) to speak in "Standard English." I do not have a problem at all with Ebonics, because most African Americans use some form of it; however, African American males also needs to know how to speak in front of people who do not speak Ebonics. By practicing this skill on a daily basis will give him a skill set that will be valuable in the future. Finally, by having the African American male to summarize his thoughts verbally this will help him to read with understanding. Oftentimes, too many of us just skim over the words in a book, but if we knew that we had to talk about what we read, we would read more intently.

In summarizing this section, we must understand that "Readers become Leaders." If we are truly looking for solution, one viable solution would be for African American males to become readers. However, this will not happen all of a sudden. It has to be intentional in the home environment. As I said at the beginning of this section, this has to be a paradigm shift in the home.

### Point #4—Developing African American Males Writing Skills

Parents, guardians, grandparents, aunts/uncles and any other caretaker, after you have developed an environment that encourages reading, we must then move it to the next level of developing the African American males writing skills. This is especially important because the world hungers for the written word. In this new millennium, we

94

have seen an increased emphasis on developing writing skills. For example, more people are using technology which requires written e-mail messages, text messages, web pages and many other forms of communication. In addition, the African American male will also need to have a command of his writing skills because he will need it to survive in society (i.e., personal business letters, papers/reports in the academic environment and even when he writes his own book about his life for others to enjoy).

The unique thing about developing writing skills is that it is inextricably tied to our previous section on reading. The more we encourage the African American male to read the better he will become at writing. Now, let's discuss some things that can be done in the home environment to improve his writing skills.

First, we need to encourage the African American male to write everyday. Writing, like any other skill, needs to be practiced to push towards perfection. Even though he may never be perfect at writing he can continue to improve his writing skills. As a result, I encourage all caretakers to have African American males summarize what they read at home verbally (based on our previous discussion) but also to express these same summaries in a written form as well. This process will help him crystallize his thoughts about what he read.

Second, he should read about places that he would like to visit one day and then write about the key points of what he learned. By reading about distant places and writing about the key points will develop writing skills that are short and succinct. This will teach him how not to waste words but to use them more productively.

Third, you should incorporate what he enjoys to improve his writing skills. As I provide professional development for educators across the United States, they are often looking for strategies that will assist them to improve the writing skills of the African American male. As a result, I came across a resource from Jawanza Kunjufu (2007) that encourages educators and/or caretakers to purchase his favorite CD (the clean version) and write down all of the lyrics. After writing the lyrics, he will then need to rewrite all of the lyrics into complete sentences (with proper subject/verb agreement) without changing the original intent of the song. By completing this activity, this will help the African American male while he is enjoying the music that he loves.

## No Grades = No Sports

In the African American community, sports play an extremely large role because many see this as one of the few avenues to "make it out the hood" and reach a life of financial prosperity. However, when I examine the data about the odds of making it into professional sports for African American males, I find that they are very slim. Please understand that I have no problem with an African American male making it to the National Basketball Association (NBA), National Football League (NFL), Major League Baseball (MLB) or any other sport but I firmly believe that he should be academically grounded just in case it does not work out. As a result, caretakers I need you to enforce the following academic golden rule of "No Grades = No Sports."

As you read this, I know for some of you that this seems a bit harsh. However, the African American male needs to know that playing sports is a privilege and academics is the first priority. Once the African American male knows that you are dedicated to this philosophy, he may not enjoy it initially but in the long-term he will greatly appreciate you for it. In some cases, the African American male may say that the coach has strict policies on grades; however, we must understand that in many cases, coaches do not follow because their main job is to win games. So, I encourage all caretakers of African American males to enforce the rule of *"No Grades = No Sports."*

## *Essential Items that must be in Every Home*

All caretakers of African American males, I have been taken extensive time reviewing research to improve the academic plight of these young men. After reviewing the latest research on this topic, I found out there are certain items that should be in every household, particularly households where African American males can thrive academically. Kunjufu (2007) reported that the following items should be readily available:

- Children's Books
- Adult Books
- Black History Books
- Library Card(s)
- Academic games (Scrabble, Checkers, Chess, UNO, Monopoly, Black History games, etc.)
- Black History Posters
- Dictionary
- Thesaurus
- Computer
- Software
- Internet Access
- Musical Instruments
- Telescope
- Chemistry Set

In examining this list, I totally agree with Dr. Kunjufu that these are items that are necessary for African Americans to thrive academically. I would encourage all caretakers to make sure that they have these items in the home but also to make sure they are being used. As we explore the various solutions for African American males, the proper utilization of these items will assist these young men to become "academic warriors" (Moore, 2003) and have a greater tenacity to pursue academic success. Further, caretakers I strongly encourage you to take time with these African American males to make sure they utilize these resources correctly. Time spent assisting the African American male to utilize these resources correctly will pay major dividends in the future.

### Solution #2 – Utilizing Community Resources

We must now move to another set of solutions that are especially important if African American males are going to improve their educational attainment. That is, the utilization of community resources. There are several that I would like to briefly discuss: (a) After-School/Weekend programs; (b) Summer Enrichment Activities; (c) Faith-Based Education programs; (d) Boys/Girls Clubs; and (e) Mentor/Mentee programs.

### After-School/Weekend Programs

Across the United States, many schools/school districts have after-school programs and/or weekend programs to meet the needs of students who may be struggling in their academic courses or would like an environment where they can spend extra time mastering their skills in a particular subject. Unfortunately, too few African American males are utilizing these resources. In most situations, these after-school/weekend programs are usually free because they are funded through various grants that the school and/or school district have received. If there is a fee, it is usually affordable in comparison to private tutoring sessions. Nevertheless, I want to encourage every caretaker who is reading this book to call their local school and/or school district and find out all of the after-school/weekend programs that are available. Once this information is obtained, if the African American male has less than stellar grades, enroll him immediately in one of these programs. Also, if the African American male wants advanced study in a particular subject, he can also utilize these programs to prepare him for future academic endeavors (i.e., college/university).

## Summer Enrichment Activities

For African American males to improve their educational attainment, they can not stop their academic pursuits at the end of the academic school year. With no academic activities for an entire summer, they are likely to forget the fundamental skills they obtained. I would encourage all caretakers to involve the African American males into some type of Summer Enrichment programs immediately following the academic school year. This will allow the African American male to continue to be in a learning environment that combines physical activities. This is especially important because most kids just lay around the house during the summer without any type of physical activity. In reflecting on my experiences, my mother enrolled me in the National Youth Sports Program (NYSP). This program combined sports (physical fitness) with academic enrichment as well. These types of activities kept me out of trouble and allowed my academic learning to continue during the summer months.

In sum, no matter which type of summer enrichment activity that you encourage the African American male to engage in is not as important as how important it is to have him doing something in the summer months. As outlined earlier in this book, many stakeholders have already calculated the numbers of African American males that will

99

die in every age category (see the intro of this book). As a result, it is critically important that the African American male is constantly involved in constructive activities, especially in the summer. We can no longer afford to have African American males just "hanging out" without anything constructive to do. As we seek transformation for the African American male, summer enrichment activities are critically important in assisting African American males to reach their goals. I encourage all caretakers to actively seek out the summer enrichment programs in your area.

### Faith-Based Education Programs

Under the administration of U.S. President George W. Bush, a significant amount of funding has been funneled into faith-based education programs. One fundamental philosophy for these funding initiatives was based on the premise that many faith-based organizations could have a greater impact in the community than the government could. As a result, many faith-based programs have obtained some of this funding to eradicate many of the social problems in their local communities.

So, as we continue to build on our discussion on improving educational attainment, many of the answers to the educational ills can be found right in these faith-based education programs. More specifically, some of these can be found in the African American Church. So, it is important to actively seek out what local faith-based programs have received this funding and explore the various options they have. Services may include free tutoring in academic areas, test-taking strategies, and many other types of educational services. These faith-based programs will continue to play a critical role in meeting the needs of the community. As a result, I encourage you to seek out these community resources and connect our African American males with these programs.

*Boy's and Girl's Clubs of America (http://www.bgca.org)*

One of the cornerstones in the African American community that has changed the lives of African Americans, particularly African American males has been the Boy's and Girl's Clubs of America. For African American males, the Boy's Club can be a valuable resource. According to the Boy's Club website (2008), the mission is to "enable all young people, especially those who need us most, to reach their full potential as productive, caring, responsible citizens." Further, the Boy's Club provides the following:

- A safe place to learn and grow;

- Ongoing relationships with caring, adult professionals;

- Life-enhancing programs and character development experiences;

- Hope and opportunity

As a young man, I attended the local Boy's Club in my community growing up. I must say that reflecting back on this experience; I now understand the impact that it had on my life. It gave me something to do, when I had nothing else to do, in a productive and caring environment.

In sum, as you read this book, the Boy's Club can be a valuable resource in assisting our African American males to have an environment that can nurture their success. I strongly encourage all caretakers of young African American males to visit their local Boy's Club to see the services they offer and utilize this great community resource.

***Big Brother/Big Sister Programs*** (http://www.bbbs.org)

One of the resources that have made a difference in the lives of African American males and many other children as well has been the Big Brother/Big Sister programs. This one-on-one mentoring program has garnered great dividends for many African American males. In reflecting on this program as a viable solution, I really feel that more African American males can have the opportunity to interact with other men who can change the direction of their lives. By promoting mentoring in a one-on-one safe environment many young African American males will have the opportunity to interact with positive African American males.

## SOLUTIONS FOR AFRICAN AMERICAN MALE ADULTS

While the majority of this chapter has focused on young African American males, I would not do this chapter proper justice if I did not provide a few thoughts on increasing the educational attainment for African American male adults. To my brothers who have picked up this book, I do want you to understand that it is never too late to improve your educational attainment. As my mother once told me, "education can take you places." As a result, I outline a few viable options that African American male adults may want to consider as they look at educational options in their future.

### *Trade Schools*

Trade Schools are probably the most under rated higher education institutions in this country. The reason I say this is they do not receive the same type of publicity as the 4-year university; however, they provide African American

102

men with a skill set that can be quite lucrative upon completion. Most trade schools have specialized programs in areas such as: welding, plumbing, A/C repair, carpentry, etc. (for more information contact your local trade school). These particular skills are in high demand in the American society. As an African American male, if you complete one of these programs, you will become a valuable employee to a company with the potential to earn a very competitive wage. Another option is to learn these skills and then start your own business, which can be even more lucrative financially. Whichever option you choose, please explore the trade school in your area as a possible avenue to increase your educational attainment.

## *Community Colleges/Junior Colleges*

For many African American males, the notion of even attending college is somewhat of a distant goal that does not seem like it can be obtained for a variety of reasons. I would suggest that if you can decide to explore the community college/junior college in your local area, this is another way you can change your life. The beauty of the community colleges/junior colleges is that many of these institutions offer many of the same programs as the trade schools. Also, they offer some of the academic programs that can be transferred to a 4-year university if you decided to attend there as well. As a result, the Community College/Junior College can provide training in a specific program (welding, carpentry, etc.) or give you the foundation in the first and second-year courses needed to transfer to a 4-year college. Even better, many of these institutions are less expensive to attend than their 4-year university counterparts.

## The Four-Year University

Last, but definitely not least, is the four-year university. I want every African American male to understand that it is never too late to explore the four-year university as an option to improve your educational attainment. The four-year university provides you with a plethora of academic majors to pursue that can have a great impact on society. Depending on the university you attend, you can explore options of attending full-time, part-time, on-line or weekend classes. Most of these universities provide an option that will possibly fit your needs.

## CONCLUSION

In this chapter, I have tried to provide some solutions to increasing the educational attainment for African American males. While I understand, this does not cover every option that is available; I wanted to at least provide some solutions for African American males whether they are a minor (under 18 years of age) or a legal adult. It is my hope that some African American males, whom I may never have the opportunity to meet, will fully digest the words of this chapter and seek to improve his educational attainment. We must remember that education is the one variable that no one can take from you. Be strong and keep the faith!

## References

Boy's Club (2019). Available at http://www.bgca.org.

Kunjufu, J. (2007). *Raising Black boys.* Chicago, IL: African American Images

# Chapter 10

# Solutions to the Unemployment and Underemployment Crisis for African American Males

*Chance W. Lewis, Ph.D.*

Solutions to the unemployment and underemployment crisis for African American males is quite a complex issue. This crisis has many layers that are quite visible and many others that are not as easily visible, and even that much harder to examine. Nevertheless, I'm sure some African American male turned to this particular chapter because they may be directly facing unemployment or underemployment issues in their own lives. Another person may have turned to this chapter because an African American male in their life is under a tremendous amount of stress because of this *dilemma*. Finally, another person may have turned to this chapter because they may want to critique what I have to say. No matter what the reason for exploring this chapter, I definitely felt God speaking to me to put just the exact words that are needed to dramatically change the life for an African American male somewhere. African American males, even though I may never meet you, I feel your pain! There are brighter days ahead because it cannot get much darker.

As a result, in this chapter, I would like to speak directly to the following individuals: (a) employers; (b) African American males who are currently unemployed (see chapter in the Issues section of this book of how I define unemployed); and (c) African American males who are underemployed. After speaking to these individuals, I would like to close out this chapter by speaking to the power players in this country who often control the jobs in this country.

## SOLUTIONS TO UNEMPLOYMENT

### Potential Employers of African American Males

Any potential employer of any African American male who has picked up this book, I want to speak directly to you. The reason I want to speak to you is because if the plight of the African American male in this country is going to change, you will play an integral part in dramatically changing the plight of these great men. We know from my writing in the earlier chapter of this book the issues of unemployment and underemployment that African American males face in this country. Further, I highlighted that African American males as a group are affected on a larger scale than males from any other race. As a result of this data, this is why I am devoting a part of this chapter to you. I ask that you strongly consider the words as I truly want to see the plight of African American males change in this country.

### Hiring Practices

Employers, I know many of you have the option, in most situations, to hire whomever you choose for positions with your respective companies, departments or whatever type of business you are involved in. Given this, I want to first break a stereotype about African American males. All African American males are NOT lazy. Of course, in every group of people you have exceptions to this rule. African American males have always been hard workers from slavery even until the present time. Many of these men want what any other person would want which is life, liberty, and the pursuit of happiness. Unfortunately, many African American males are not being provided with the opportunity to work productively on a job for a variety of reasons. Nevertheless, I just want to focus in on how we can improve the hiring practices of African American males.

First, when an African American male fills out an application for employment, in many cases, he is paper-screened out of the position immediately. This means based on his name sounding like a "Black Name," in many cases his application is put in a DO NOT HIRE file. Right at this point, I am asking each employer reading this chapter to review the hiring practices to bring about a solution to this type of discrimination that goes on quite frequently in this country. We must remember a person's name is not an indication of what type of employee they can become. So, please, provide the African American male with a fair opportunity in the application process to even make it through the application process.

Second, employers should take the time to understand the nature of background checks. Employers you know that when you run background checks on all your applicants, the nature of these reports are sometimes simple and other times very complicated. Unfortunately, in most situations, African American male applications are greatly affected by these background checks. Nevertheless, I would strongly urge employers to take time to thoroughly review the nature of the background check reports before jumping to conclusions about the capabilities of any applicant, particularly African American males. If this report documents that this African American male was arrested and convicted of a misdemeanor crime and served jail time, you must ask yourself if he has paid his debt to society and completed all necessary requirements to be eligible for employment, why should he be punished again, if he is a quality applicant for the position? Often times, many African American males are passed over for many employment opportunities because of their past; however, I am advocating that employers give these applicants a second look to prove himself because truth be told, we have all done something that we are not proud of.

I know some employers reading this section are saying that I did not address African American males who have convicted of felony offenses that ultimately show up on their criminal record. In certain types of jobs (e.g., schools, certain government positions, etc.) persons with felony convictions are not allowed to work at these types of jobs. These are not the jobs I am referring to. There are many positions, where a person with a felony conviction can work and not harm anyone. We must remember that this could be the one job that can change his life around and all he needs is just the opportunity to show what he can do. It is no need for an African American male who has a felony conviction, who has successfully paid his debt to society, not to get an opportunity to feed his family. If we are going to have solutions, we must not design a system within our companies that perpetuate sending this African American male back into the prison system. So, I conclude this section, I am asking employers to examine their hiring practices to make sure they are fair and equitable for African American males to even have an opportunity to be gainfully employed!

### Overcoming the Stereotype of Hiring the African American Male

Employers in the United States society, there are a variety of stereotypes of the African American male. Many of these stereotypes I have highlighted in the preface of this book. To this end, I know that there are ways for the African American male to overcome some of the *dilemmas* he currently faces will be for people (employers and others in positions of authority) to overcome their stereotypes of what they feel about the African American male. More specifically, employers, I would like for you to examine an African American male and any other applicant, in the words of Rev. Dr. Martin Luther King, Jr., by the "content of their character." As I mentioned in the preface of this book, all African American males are not thugs, gang bangers, athletes or entertainers, many of these men want the same basic things out of life that everyone else wants which is life, liberty, and the pursuit of happiness.

Second, employers also need to look past some of their individual perceptions of what they think the African American male represents. I know in many situations that certain jobs come down to 2-3 applicants and ultimately it is up to the employer or the designated hiring official to make a "judgment call" about who they will hire. In most situations, some African American men are not viewed in a favorable light when these types of judgment calls need to be made. As a result of these behind closed door decisions, many African American males are left without a job to ultimately take care of their families. So, as we seek solutions in this chapter, I want to have any employer who is reading this chapter to give the African American male a "second look" in those types of decisions that are made behind closed doors. By doing so, unemployment and underemployment issues can be greatly reduced if African American males are given a fair opportunity to obtain gainful employment.

Finally, I am asking all employers to conduct a self-examination and decide if they have contributed to the *dilemmas* that African American males face in the areas of unemployment and underemployment. As the old saying goes, "if you are not part of the solution...you are part of the problem." This is why I ask that you really take on this self-examination. I must say that it is funny how this world is setup; our money (taxes we pay) can be used to emancipate people from their conditions or continue to oppress them in their conditions. Employers, either way, your tax dollars will be used to either enhance the plight of the African American male or continue to oppress them. I must say that when people are oppressed and they learn that they are oppressed, they will resort to any necessary means to survive. As a result, I ask from the bottom of my heart; if the African American male is qualified for a job, give him a serious look. Do not dismiss him from the opportunity just because of how he looks. Also, do not dismiss him because of his criminal record if you are not doing the same for other persons in the applicant pool. All I am asking for is fairness in the job hiring process so *dilemmas* of unemployment and underemployment can be eradicated in the African American community. If African American males are able to obtain gainful employment, crime in the African American community will greatly decrease. Let's start today employers with solutions to unemployment and underemployment for African American males.

### *African American Males who are Unemployed*

This section of the chapter is dedicated to all the African American males who are able to work, who want to work, but are currently unable to find work. Most in society would say that you are unemployed. I want to say you are on the verge of your breakthrough. In this portion of the chapter and the solutions to the Economic *dilemmas* chapter, I want to help to lead you to your breakthrough. I ask that you walk with me through a few thoughts God has put in my head that will lead you to a path of life transformation.

### *This is not the end…it's the beginning*

My brother, I want you to clearly understand that just because you are unemployed your world is not about to come to an end. You must understand that God sees you and has many more blessings for your life. In the previous sections of this chapter, I have spoken to potential employers of how they need to promote fairness in their hiring practices. However, I want to speak to you in your unemployment situation. You must truly have faith that God does not want you in this situation. You must be ready to position yourself to receive this blessing. This is when faith is tested, when things are not going according to plan.

I must say that while you are "in-between" jobs you do not do anything that goes against God's Will for your life. This could include resorting to drugs, alcohol, or any substance to try to ease the pain of unemployment or not being able to provide for your family. As I attempt to focus you to bring solutions to the unemployment *dilemmas* that you currently face, now is the time for us to do a few things that will prepare you for your next job (really your next breakthrough from God). They are as follows:

(a) developing an action plan to find gainful employment;

(b) adding additional skills to your current skill set;

(c) marketing your skills to your potential employer;

(d) overcoming previous criminal records

### Developing an Action Plan to Find Gainful Employment

One of the most important elements in finding gainful employment is to develop an action plan and knowing how to effectively look for gainful employment. This is a key element that will move you on a path to finding the type of job that is right for you. I want to encourage every African American male reading this book who is unemployed to intently study the "employment section" of your local newspaper and find the local employment offices in your area. These two resources have a wealth of resources that can provide you with information on the types of jobs that are available in your area. Once you have accessed this information, I want you to make a listing of all the jobs available that fit your skills. This will give you a "job pool" to target as we seek future employment.

The next step I would like you to do is intently study these job announcements and make another list of the jobs that you are "most qualified" to apply for based on your previous job skills, education, etc. We will call this our job target list. So, now you should have two lists, "potential jobs" and "job target lists."

Next, all of the positions on your job target list, I want you to find out the types of things you need to apply for each of these positions. You may see the following requirements: (a) a formal letter of application; (b) a resume'; (c) letters of recommendation; (d) a writing sample; (e) a portfolio, etc. I want you to start gathering this information so we can move to formally applying for these positions.

At this point, I want you to involve other people you can trust to review your application materials. Pull the applications for these positions and start to fill these out in either black ink or have the application typed based on what the potential employer prefers. All materials (resume', letter of application, etc.) should be typewritten with no punctuation or spelling errors. These documents will give the potential employer a first-hand view of how you present yourself.

Based on the second list that we formulated, we are not ready to submit the application materials to the prospective employers. Before we do so, I ask that you find you some clothing that makes you look "presentable." For some types of jobs, this could be a suit; for other types of jobs this could be when you dress in business casual attire. No matter which type of job it is, I ask that you look "presentable" and go to the job location and hand deliver your materials. The rationale behind this is that now the human resources personnel at this job location can associate a face with the application materials. This is really important because your application will not have the same effect if it is just arriving in the mail. Another added benefit to hand-delivering your application materials is that whomever is doing the hiring may have a few minutes to briefly speak with you about the position. Remember, this will probably not be the interview but this will be a few minutes to speak about why you feel you are the best person for this job. So, as you develop your action plan, you must be prepared on the types of things you want to say about yourself or your skills if afforded the opportunity to speak to the hiring official.

## *The Job Interview*

After you submit your application materials, if the company you are seeking to work for has a genuine interest in you, they usually set up an appointment for a formal job interview. Brothers, you have to look at this as an opportunity to sell yourself and the skills you can bring to the job for your prospective employer. On the day of your job interview, I would highly suggest that you arrive early, looking nice and have additional copies of your application materials (letter of application, resume', etc.). When they are ready to begin the interview, they will usually invite you to come into the designated place where they will conduct the interviews. I suggest you provide a "firm" handshake to all the people that will be interviewing you. You should quickly decipher if they want you to call them by their first names or more formal title like Mr. or Ms.

As you proceed through the interview, the prospective employer will be interviewing what you say and how you look when you say it (your dispositions). This is why I suggest that you be confident (not cocky) as you speak in the interview. Oftentimes, many people lose opportunities because they are not very confident in what they are speaking about. Also, as you are in this interview, your answers should show that you have done your research on the company. Also, you should also try to weave in some information on the people that are interviewing you as well. By knowing background on the company and on the interviewers, you are able to frame your answers in the best way possible to set you up to be successful in the interview.

Another strategy that is very important is to ask questions at the end of the interview. Oftentimes, the interviewers will say, do you have any questions for us? You should always have well-informed questions. However, I would refrain from discussing pay at this point because this usually turns the interviewers off. Your questions may be framed as to give you more clarification of maybe something said in the interview or some policies/procedures on the job. No matter what type of questions you ask, please make sure they are well-informed. Finally, after your questions, I would suggest that you close the interview thanking the interviewers for their time in providing you with an interview and how excited you are about the possibility of working with their company.

## SOLUTIONS TO UNDEREMPLOYMENT

For the African American males reading this book who feel they are underemployed, I provide this section for you. Many Americans feel like they are undervalued on their jobs and they are not getting paid what they are worth. As a result, frustration sets in and unfortunately, they do not perform as best as they can because of their feelings of importance on the job. In most situations, underlying feelings of underemployment are financial issues (I'm not getting paid what I'm worth.). As a result, I will briefly address how you can increase your pay at your job.

In addressing this section, my research allowed me to come across a book entitled, *Start Late, Finish Rich* (David Bach, 2005/2018) and in this book he describes a 4-week plan to getting a pay raise. I would encourage everyone to read this section of the book as it can be life-changing. However, to provide solutions to underemployment issues, he provides several general questions that I feel are important for this section of the chapter (Bach, 2005, p. 178) that you need to ask yourself if you want to move from being underemployed to a valued employee:

- As an employee, do you stand out or blend in?
- If you left the company, would it be hurt or helped?
- Do you come to work on time, early, or late?
- Do you have a written plan for your career that describes how you add value at work, or do you wing it?
- Do you have a relationship with a person who determines whether you should get a raise?
- Do you know anything about his or her family?
- Does he or she know anything about your family?
- Do you really care about the company you work for or is it just a job?
- Do you spend any time, money and/or effort learning new job skills so you can add greater value to your company?
- Do you have a vision of where you want to be with your employer in 3-5 years?
- Does your employer know you have a vision?

African American males, as you look at these questions, they should be revealing to you as you look at yourself and examine why you may be underemployed. Oftentimes, we always like to look at external factors but it is those internal factors that we bring to the table that hold us back. So, as we seek the solutions for underemployment, you should write down where you want to be to reverse your situation (Bach, 2005/2018). More specifically, you should develop an action plan (see Bach, 2018, p. 179).

To move your action plan forward, Bach (2005/2018) asks the following seven major questions:

1. What is the most important thing I do for my boss?
2. What does my boss think that I'm uniquely talented at?
3. What would my boss be afraid to tell me about my job and how I do it?
4. What would by boss say I could do to add more value to my job?
5. What could I do to be my boss's "dream team" employee?
6. Knowing what he or she has learned about me in all the time I've worked here, would my boss hire me today?
7. What would my boss say it would take for me to get a raise in the next 6 months?

In conclusion, to help solve some of the underemployment issues that plague African American males in the workforce, we need first to look at how we can honestly answer the seven questions previously mentioned. If we can answer all of the questions in the affirmative than it is warranted that you sit down and have a conversation with your employer and be ready to document how you are an asset to your company and why you deserve a pay raise and/or a new position within the company. It is my prayer that one day all African American males can receive the necessary educational training to stimulate their minds and achieve new heights in various career trajectories. May God send supernatural blessings your way!

References

Bach, D. (2005/2018). *Start late, finish rich.* New York: Broadway.

*"A life is not important except in the impact it has*

*on other lives."*

**Jackie Robinson**

# Chapter 11

# Overcoming Substance Abuse and Reclaiming your Life

"There is no doubt in my mind that there are many ways to be a winner, but there is really only one way to be a loser and that is to fail and not look beyond one's failure." - Kyle Rote, Jr.

*Kris F. Erskine, Th.D.*

We would want to believe that we live in a world where if you ignored problems they would just go away. But, the question I pose is: "What if you constantly live with the problem?" The pandemic known as substance abuse is not only destroying individual lives, but also the fibers of the family unit. This growing problem is rearing its head earlier and earlier as generations are faced with the decision whether to use or not. My battle with substance abuse is totally different from the normal horrific stories of the abuser, but rather the blind family member. The family member who was driven down the abyss of abuse thinking all was well and it was their problem or it can be fixed. The family member who bought the fuel for the ride never asked why you are doing this to yourself. Enabling is the word we avoid because it draws us back into the equation we desperately try to escape. I have lived the greater portion of my life assisting people who are abusers.

The one element that I must share immediately is that there is **no addiction** that cannot be conquered. The ingredients to conquer this addiction is altogether something else. The drive and the mental fortitude that is demanding of all involved is greater than some are willing cosign to see it conquered. From rehabs to rehabs and from programs to programs, this is a life cycle that you must be willing to commit to before you sign up for the process. Half hearted dedication will only produce more pain. It will cause the abuser to give up on hope and resolve that they are going to die in their addiction. The choice to start is the center of where overcoming begins. You must be willing to walk back down the deserted streets and alleys of the past of the abuser and carefully listen to them explain how they were introduced to their addiction who was a distant stranger who has now become a trusted friend. It is taxing to see someone you love struggle within as it is visible without. The secret pains we endure are ripping enough. Then add the eyes of the world watching you as trying keep balance to a top heavy addiction. But, you can overcome!

You can become what I believe is an "Overcomer." The Bible records in Revelations 12:11- "And they overcame him (the enemy, addiction, depression, death) by the blood of the lamb and by the word of their testimony; and they loved not their lives unto death." In this one scripture, I believe lays the formula for freedom from anything and anyone. When you dissect this text, the enemy here is represented by satan, the devil, evil forces and/or addictions. His job is to go before God day and night and accuse us of the wrong that he enticed us to enter in. The afflicted regained their purpose after he is cast down from the place of prominence that we provide him. We then continue to conquer by what is implied by the scripture above - the constant relationship with God and confession from our own mouths, as well as wanting deliverance and freedom more than we wanted to live. There is a story told of a young man who asked an older man for wisdom. The two where fishing in a boat on a sunny day. The old, white head gentleman asked the bright eyed and green young man "how bad do you want it." Very badly exclaimed the young man!

The old man told him to hold his head over the side of the boat. The young man looked puzzled, but obeyed. Without warning the older man took his head and pushed it down into the water and held it for a few seconds and then released it. Gasping for breath, the young man asked "What are you trying to do, kill me." No he said. Just checking to see how bad you want it. I want it bad screamed the young man! Hold your head over the side of the boat again then. "What! No way, said the young man. If you wanted it bad enough you would. With some hesitation, he positioned his head back over the side. The older gentleman pushed his head down holding it a little longer than before. When he released the young man's head, dripping water everywhere, he shouted, "What are you crazy?" No replied the older gentleman. "How bad do you want it?" I want it bad, but. But what, said the older gentleman! Hold your head over here again. No sir, screamed the young man. You are going to push my head in the water again. The older gentleman said "Now, is wisdom knocking on the door of your mind." But, to open the door and allow wisdom to come in, you must want it worst than you wanted you next breath while your head was under water.

The young man smiled and said, "Now I understand." You must desire change like the next breath you are going to breathe. Start developing your relationship with God. The same God you cried out to for freedom. The same God you needed like the young man in the previous story. Stop making excuses and stop feeling shame and sorrow about your past. It is done. You cannot cry over spilled milk my grandmother used to say, clean it up! For those of you on the other side of addiction, stop enabling them. You justify it by saying it is not a lot of money or if I don't help them who will. But, driving the get-away car is just as guilty as the one robbing the bank. You are supplying them with access as they hurriedly rob themselves of life. One of the most complex things is to say no to people you love and/or want to love. But the damage you do to them is worse than the substance they are abusing. To reap the rewards of rehabilitation and overcome you must be willing to share. Share what you may be asking. Share your story. Who would really want to hear about my story you are probably asking? It will amaze you who will listen to you. People gravitate to people who speak truth about what they struggle with. I don't have the right words. I cannot look at people. I cannot face people. All of these are road blocks in the path of your success. Go over them slow and try it.

John Maxwell once said; "What happened to you is not the most important thing, what happened in you is." Confession speaks about what happened not to you but in you. What changed and how did you handle it? What mistakes can you now appreciate? Who did you hurt in the process? How do you feel now? Why would you never use again? Three things that this addiction taught you that you will never forget. Three things you cannot get back. Name something that the addiction could not rob you of. It is amazing that each person I worked with have something that they are able to say that the addiction could not take from them. These things may be hidden deep down within you. But, trust me it is there. Confession will allow you to cleanse your mind. Talking about your pain has medicine in it. It begins to eliminate the pain the more you talk about it. With each sentence you release an area of your life that was sentenced to death while battling the addiction.

Most psychologists agree that any form of expression is the starting point to recovery. What you will not confront, you will never conquer. Lastly, the scripture implies that they loved not their lives unto death. They were willing to do whatever it would take to get better. Are you at this point in your life? Willing to do **"whatever"** it will cost of you. Embrace the support that comes from others in small group meetings and one-on-one mentoring sessions. You cannot do this alone. Addiction tried to rob you everyone of essence in your life. The process of addiction is to move a person to an island of loneliness. This is an island where the only companions are depression and death. Now, that you have made up your mind to reclaim your life, share your story and allow others to share their support. I must admit that this is a life long struggle and battle. There will never be a day that you do not battle. Each day will be better than previous, but battles never cease. You must develop what one my mentors refer to as a "new normal." It is the normalcy you desire or the one you may be accustomed to. But it speaks directly to where you are right now. The struggle will allow you to remain humble in the healing process.

As your transition into the "new you" or the "you right now," understand that you are not what you do and/or have done! The events of our lives though hurtful and painful are yet purposeful. In your transitioning period, I want to share an article that I was grateful to write in the Bryan-College Station Eagle Newspaper- May 17th, 2008. It speaks vividly on the subject of transition and how to overcome. Each year I am privileged to sit in Reed Arena on the campus of Texas A&M University and watch promising individuals receive their degrees. As a pastor in a transitional town, I have accepted the fact that we have only a few moments to make lifelong impressions on people's lives. At this time last year, I wrote an article called "Breaking the Holding Pattern." It examined how, in life, we are cumbered by patterns and seasons when seemingly we are going nowhere fast. During this same season of transition, I would like to offer some points of purpose.

Jesus, in Mark 10:46-52, pulls back pages of Scripture to allow us to meet a man named Bartimaeus. This man was blind, a beggar and banished to the side of the road. His life had been placed on pause because of the vicissitudes of life. Many of you reading this article can identify with Bartimaeus because you, too, are on the sideline of life. You are meandering on a path of no activity, no productivity and no excitement. Why is life so complex? Like Bartimaeus, you must be ready for transition. I have often used this quote by Leonard Ravenhill, the late Christian evangelist: "The opportunity of a lifetime must be seized within the lifetime of the opportunity." Get in the right position for opportunity even when situated on the sideline of life. Get in the right position mentally. Expect better, and better will begin to gravitate to you. Think better thoughts, read better books and speak better words! Bartimaeus -- blind, begging and banished -- knew that when Jesus of Nazareth would be passing by, he had to seize the opportunity. He might never see this opportunity again. When Jesus grew closer to where he was, the Bible records that Bartimaeus began to shout, "Jesus of Nazareth. Have mercy on me! Jesus, Jesus of Nazareth.

Have mercy on me!" **Bartimaeus overcame the outlook hindering him.** Like Bartimaeus, you can no longer afford to be silent in a sinking and sorrowful situation. When I'm frustrated, a good yell, scream and/or shout will allow me to process better. Release is a form of therapy that removes the cloudy and promotes clarity. It is interesting that the gospel passage records that the people who could see Jesus were silent and that they had a problem with the blind man who would not keep quiet. The story of Bartimaeus first instructs us never to be silenced by life's outlook. And, second, we learn from Bartimaeus what we should do next. **He overcame the opinions about him.** The crowds of people began to shout at him, "Be quiet!" The religious will always tell the radical that it does not take all of that, that the radical is too extreme. Yet the religious did not have the need that Bartimaeus had, so they were not required to be as demonstrative as he was. How badly do you need Jesus?

Do not allow the opinions of others to cement you in life's circumstances. It was Edward Gibbon who said, "I never make the mistake of arguing with people for whose opinions I have no respect."

But what the seeing crowd felt about Bartimaeus did not hinder Jesus from healing him. What people feel about you will not hinder God from blessing you, either. The opinions of others will catapult or corral you. The choice is yours. Finally, a last lesson from Bartimaeus: He did what I believe was the hardest of them all. **He overcame the obstacles blocking him.** The Bible records that when Jesus came near him, the Savior heard how emphatically the blind man was screaming for him. Your desire should cause you to become passionate about whatever your purpose is tied to. Jesus stood still and told the people who had tried to quiet Bartimaeus to escort the blind man to him. At that precise moment, the Bible records that Bartimaeus cast away his garment and came to Jesus! What an awesome statement. There must be something in your life that is blocking you from moving forward in life. Bartimaeus instructs us to cast it to the side. After looking at Bartimaeus, Jesus engaged in dialogue with the man of desperation. "What is it that you will I do for you?" Jesus offered to help Bartimaeus, providing him with the opportunity of a lifetime -- and he will do the same for you in transition!

## 2nd Edition Reflections

This last section of this presentation for me serves bitter sweet. Overcoming Substance Abuse and Reclaiming your Life is a daily battle for so many men of culture and color. The systemic substance abuse recovery is regulated to the culture the addict. Many find themselves eager to enter the process of recovery, but lack the culture and communal support for success. In this sense, stress, confusion, and a desire for peer acceptance all seem to play a role in substance abuse during the acculturation process. During this cultural balancing act, individuals may fall in with peer groups that hold different values than those of their family and, in many cases, may condone substance use as a part of their subculture (Grand Canyon University, 2008). Balancing and embracing these two cultural contexts can be challenging and stressful. These sets of stresses can trigger alcohol and other drug use as a way of self-medicating and seeking relief (Grand Canyon University, 2008; Matheson & McGrath, Jr., 2012).

The importance of Overcoming Substance Abuse and Reclaiming your Life is rooted in a healthy and commitment to the psychology of recovery. The mind changes the lifestyle. The lifestyle is subject to impulses and influence of the mind. One's cultural reality weighs heavy on their psychosis. Many inner city and urban communities are bombarded with billboards that support the sale and use of alcohol and drugs.

This is not only detrimental, but also devastating to a successful recovery. One will never recover from any addiction until the mind is fully committed to change with cultural support. The effectiveness of treatment and prevention programs depends on their ability to reach out into the communities to determine the needs of the individuals in that community and, thus, tailor the services available accordingly (Castro & Alcaron, 2002).

Instead of taking a blind approach to offering services, prevention and treatment programs can become aware of the needs of individuals and their families in the community and offer viable, effective services to address their unique needs. The needs of one neighborhood are most likely entirely different from those of another and this must be taken into consideration if professionals seek to establish and maintain culturally relevant and effective services.

Overcoming Substance Abuse and Reclaiming your Life is a proactive role that supports the individual and the community at large. The decision to make a change is the initial step in this process. Here is a list of other value steps provided by the alcohol-rehab.com:

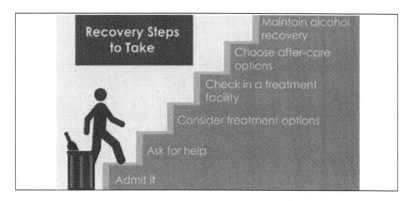

Recovery.org provides great tools for Overcoming Substance Abuse and Reclaiming Your Life through:

**4 Lifestyle Changes That Can Help With Recovery**

Breaking habits often requires changing the way you think, as well as changing behavioral patterns that have developed over the years. Some changes you can make include:

*Learn new strategies for stress management. Spend time with people who do not use drugs or alcohol.

*Find new ways to spend your free time.

*Change the way you feel about yourself.

Finally, here are some valuable resources that one can implement immediately.

**Resources**

**The National Alliance on Mental Illness** provides information and resources for African Americans on a wide range of mental health issues. The organization also offers tips for how to find a culturally competent treatment provider.

**Drugs, Alcohol, and HIV/AIDS**: A Consumer Guide for African Americans is a pamphlet published by the Substance Abuse and Mental Health Services Administration (SAMHSA) that explains the risks of contracting HIV and AIDS among African Americans who abuse drugs and alcohol. The pamphlet also provides information on what to do if you have been diagnosed with HIV or AIDS.

**Keeping Your Teens Drug-Free:** A Guide for African American Parents and Caregivers offers information on the dangers of teen drug use and tips for parents on preventing and helping teens who have already begun experimenting with drugs and alcohol.

**Alcoholics Anonymous (AA)** provides support for anyone who is addicted to alcohol and has a desire to quit drinking. Meetings are available in over 170 countries in several different languages. For more information on how AA can help African Americans struggling with alcoholism, see A.A. for the Black and African American Alcoholic.

# References

Hamlet- by Shakespeare

**Jeff Herring** - EzineArticles.com Expert Author

Brainy Quotes.com- **Antoine de Saint-Exupery**

**Who    Moved    My    Cheese-**Spencer    Johnson

Inspirational Quotes- Lao Tzu

Kris F. Erskine- Bryan-College Station Eagle Newspaper (May 17th issue)

*"Racism is not an excuse to not do the best you can."*

*Arthur Ashe*

# Chapter 12

# Get Your Money—The Right Way: Solutions to the Economic Issues Impacting African American Males

*Chance W. Lewis, Ph.D.*

We have reached the last chapter that we will explore in Part I of our *dilemma* series of issues impacting African American males. In this chapter, I would like to talk specifically to African American males about strategies need so you can strive to get your money the right way. In the U.S., we are fortunate to have many ways to get paid if we are willing to "think outside of the box" or as others would put it, to think strategically. Unfortunately, many African American males are not using their God-given talent to get paid legally in this society. As a result, we find many African American males falling into what is called the Cradle-to-the-Prison pipeline (I provided a discussion on this earlier in this book).

This chapter for me is probably one of my most passionate as I want each of you to prosper in all areas of your life. However, it is important for you to reach your financial potential because this impacts so many other areas of your life. So, it is my hope that this chapter provides you with what you need to get your money the right way.

### *Your Choice: Legal or Illegal Money*

African American males, I want you to understand that you have a choice of how you seek to receive your money over your life span. Basically, it comes down to this, the money you are receiving, is it legal or illegal? For the sake of

131

clarification, legal money are funds that you receive that you will not be arrested for receiving if someone were to investigate you. On the opposite end of the spectrum, illegal money is money you receive that is not in alignment with the laws of the United States. Basically, you cannot really blur the lines (many people still try to) on this issue because the money is either legally or illegally gained.

I do want you to understand that the path you choose to gain your money directly deals with two important issues that you need to consider: (a) Quality of life and (b) Ramifications for future generations. So, let's deal with the first issue—Quality of Life.

### *Quality of Life*

African American males, when you make the choice about how you choose to receive your money, you also have just made a decision about the quality of life you choose to have as well. What I mean by quality of life is what I call the "sleep at night" factor. If you choose to receive your money illegally, you have greatly impacted your 'sleep at night' factor because you now have to be on constant guard that someone may come and possibly put bullet holes in your place of residence because of something that has gone wrong with the illegal activities that you are participating in. I know most African American males think it will never happen to them; however, in this day and age you never now. Also, you put your family members and neighbors in harm's way because of your decision to receive your money illegally. It is not fair for innocent people to be hurt because of decisions you have made. However, if you choose this life style, you will never have peace because you will always know in the back of your mind that someone may want retribution "any time of the day or night" and sooner or later this will have an impact on your quality of life.

On the flip side, if you choose to receive your money through a legal way, you will not have the same type of issues as described previously. The reason is that since you have made this choice, your 'sleep at night" factor is much more peaceful because you know that you have not engaged in any activity where someone will want retribution for something that you have done where they will come by your place of residence to carry out any violent acts. As a result, your family and neighbors can live in a much calmer state and know that their place of residence that you have provided is really 'home sweet home.'

### Ramifications for Future Generations of Your Family

African American males, I want you to know that your choices of how you get your money have ramifications for future generations of your family. I want you to understand that if you make a decision to get your money illegally, you also have just set an example for your children, nephews, nieces, and other family members of how they should get their money. You must remember that you do not know who is looking up to you as a role model. This is how so many males in the African American community make bad choices because they are emulating the lives of people they really look up to. As a result, the negative cycle starts one, two, three or more generations of men and women in one family who decide to get their money the wrong way. It is your choice!!

### Get Your Money the Right Way: What Needs to Happen?

### Step 1: Obtain Legal Employment

African American males, no matter your current age, I strongly urge you to pursue employment that is legal for a

133

variety of reasons. First, as I mentioned earlier in this chapter, you will have accomplished the 'sleep at night' factor because you are not worried about someone coming to your place of residence to harm you because of illegal activity. Second, you will obtain a certain pride about yourself. To put it plainly, there is a certain pride that you carry when you go to work on a legal job to support your family. Even if the job is not the best job for you, at least you have something that is bringing in income that can support your financially. Third, when you obtain legal employment, you put yourself in the arena of other people who are doing things in a legal way. Remember the old saying, "Birds of a feather flock together." Fourth, one legal job can lead to a better legal job. We must remember that when people seek to possibly hire you for a position, they like to examine your work history. In examining your work history, if they found out you have a pattern of not seeking legal employment over a particular time span; it will raise a concern in their eyes. Finally, when you obtain legal employment, it allows you to legally save money for your future and the future of your family. This in itself should motivate you to pursue legal employment.

### Step 2: Develop an Entrepreneurial Passion while you Work on Your Job

For this section of the chapter, I really want to encourage all African American males at all stages of life to develop an entrepreneurial spirit. However, I want to revitalize us to pursue entrepreneurial ventures but we must be smarter and not just quit our current job in order to pursue the big risk of entrepreneurship. I am a firm believer that the foundation of your new business can be built while are still on your current job. For example, all of the background work (reading, studying, identifying your target market) should be done while on your current job. Also, depending on the type of business you are pursuing you can probably establish this while still working as well. So, as we venture into this territory of entrepreneurship, I want you to explore a few things as you consider this option.

## *What are you good at?*

African American males, if you want to become an entrepreneur, you have to understand what skills would be of benefit to someone else. I would suggest that you really go through a process of self-reflection so you can clearly identify what skill set you have that you can start an entrepreneurial business with. It is amazing to me that many people, African American males included, have so many skills but are so nervous, scared, or timid to step out into entrepreneurship. It is my opinion, that we are always taught to just find a 'good job' that entrepreneurship is always put on the backburner. Nevertheless, I want you to find what skills you have that can be turned into a business opportunity. If you like mowing lawns, this skill could be a potential business for you. Do you like computers? That can be another business opportunity as well. No matter what it is, you must have faith to be able to turn this into a business.

## *Do You Have a Passion to be an Entrepreneur?*

African American males, another critical point that must be explained, if you are going to get your money the right way, is to be very passionate about your business. This is especially important because as you move into entrepreneurship, you will be faced with many hurdles and your passion for this business will be the one thing that will get you through this time. So, as you consider entrepreneurship, I would pose the one question about this venture. How passionate are you about the business you want to start? Do you have enough passion about this business to keep going if you face tough times in this business? These questions pertaining to passion are extremely important if you want to get your money the right way?

### Are You Filling a Need in the Community?

After you have examined your skills and your passion, the next item I want you to examine before stepping into entrepreneurship are the needs of your community. This step is important and many entrepreneurs neglect this step because they are just focused on themselves. However, you can have skills and passion, but if you do not have a clear assessment of what your community needs how do you know they will serve as customers for your business? This is why I clearly want you to scan your community to make sure that it can benefit from what you are providing. Also, you should also know if there are similar businesses as the one that you are planning to start. If there are similar businesses in the community, you should know everything about them and how your business will be different to benefit your customers. Remember, your homework is essential if you are going to be successful at entrepreneurship.

### Step 3: Decide to Do It! Don't Procrastinate!

As we have taken this journey through this chapter, I strongly urge you to not procrastinate if you really want to start your own business. Many African Americans, particularly African American males who wanted to start their own business have failed because of one main negative characteristic—procrastination. This one word is a disease in the African American community. However, as a result of reading this chapter, I want to strongly encourage you to not procrastinate on your idea. Start putting your plans into action. Set up your business legally, open up a business account at your local back and become

OFFICIAL. If you are going to go into business for yourself, be professional and run it properly. In future books in this *dilemma* series, I will get more into the details, but for now, DECIDE TO DO IT! DON'T PROCRASTINATE!

## CONCLUSION

In conclusion, I have attempted to provide a general overview of how you can get your money the right way. We live in a country with so many opportunities to get paid from a variety of sources. However, for many of us, we are bound by a spirit of procrastination. However, now is the time for us to transform our communities by exploring entrepreneurship. I must tell you that there is no other pride like working for yourself. Honestly, if you are working on a job, you can still work for yourself on the side utilizing the main skills that you have. Please remember, I do not want you to limit yourself. Step out on faith and start some kind of business where one day you can pass it down to those who will come behind you.

# Epilogue

*Chance W. Lewis, Ph.D. and Kris F. Erskine, Th.D.*

It has been a great pleasure writing this book. It is our hope that this book will reach someone, particularly African American males, who are dealing with a plethora of *dilemmas* in their lives. While we could not cover every *dilemma* possible, we decided to provide chapters focused on solutions for each of the *dilemmas* presented. For each of us, this is just the starting point of what God has planted in us. As a result, we have planned to start a book series around various *dilemmas* that African Americans (males and females) face on a daily basis. So, we ask that you be on the look out for our future books in this series.

For more information, you can visit the personal webpage of Dr. Chance W. Lewis at http://www.chancewlewis.com and you can visit Dr. Kris Erskine at http://www.themovementdaily.org.

# ABOUT THE AUTHORS

Chance W. Lewis, Ph.D. is a Distinguished Professor of Urban Education and Director of The Urban Education Collaborative at the University of North Carolina at Charlotte. Additionally, Dr. Lewis is the Provost Faculty Fellow for Diversity, Inclusion and Access at UNC Charlotte. Also, Dr. Lewis is President/CEO of Lewis Educational Consultants (http://www.chancewlewis.com), a consulting firm dedicated to improving the educational attainment of students of color in our nation's public schools. Dr. Lewis can be reached by e-mail at chance.lewis@gmail.com.

Kris F. Erskine, Th.D. is Senior Pastor of Operations at Bethel Missionary Baptist Church, Pratt City in Birmingham, Alabama. Dr. Erskine is President of The Movement Daily (http://www.themovementdaily.org) that is committed to providing life solutions to those oppressed in life's struggles. Dr. Erskine can be reached email at pastorerskine@aol.com.

Made in the USA
Columbia, SC
16 October 2022

69522389R00085